FROM THE AUTHOR

This book has been produced and copied from its original hardcover form. At that time the prime was 6%. There are references in Chapters 2, 3, 4 and 30 as well as Client Chapter 5 to concepts that involve borrowing from a stock brokerage firm at Broker Call Rates or from Banks at Libor Rates. These figures now range between 7% and 8.5% instead of the original 5%. This will change the figures slightly, but not the concepts. They still work, only the cost may be slightly higher.

There is a further reference to a guaranteed drop in the stock market in Chapter 10. The market has since moved from 3,700 to 6,000. With this concept I show the stock market will "crash 2,000 points guaranteed" and those figures should be changed to 3,300 points, representing a 55% drop of the stock market on the day you die, since 55% of your assets will go to Uncle Sam, in estate taxes. The concepts remain the same in all situations, only the numbers may be different.

There are three new concepts that I would like to allude to:

1. "Tax deductible" loans to purchase insurance with no payment until your death
2. Increase your exemptions up to $24 million
3. Turn any estate tax into an asset

These ideas are alluded to in *Die Rich and Tax Free*. However, they are detailed completely in my new book, *The Investment Alternative*, which will be finished later in 1997. If you have any questions about any of the changes outlined above or ideas or concepts explained in the book, do not hesitate to call me for a complete explanation at 800-DIE-RICH (800-343-7424).

Other Books by Barry Kaye

$2.7 Million In My First Year, 1963
How To Save A Fortune On Your Life Insurance, 1981
Save A Fortune On Your Estate Taxes, 1990
Live Rich, 1996

DIE RICH AND TAX FREE

by Barry Kaye

Dearborn
Financial Publishing, Inc.®

Published by Dearborn Financial Publishing, Inc.®

98 99 10 9 8 7 6 5 4 3 2

Library of Congress Cataloging-in-Publication Data

Kaye, Barry, 1928–
     Die rich and tax free / by Barry Kaye.
        p.   cm.
     Includes index.
     ISBN 0-7931-2489-1
     1. Inheritance and transfer tax—Law and legislation—United States—Popular works.   2. Insurance, Life—Taxation—Law and legislation—United States—Popular works.   3. Estate planning—United States.   I. Title.
     KF6588.Z9K39   1997
     343.7305'32—dc21   96-52847
                                                           CIP

Dedication

I dedicate this book to the professionals in America—the attorneys, accountants, trust officers, insurance people, financial planners—in the hopes that they'll develop a better understanding of some of the wealth creation and preservation techniques contained within it for the ultimate benefit of their clients.

I dedicate the concepts presented within this book to the American public as a whole that they may, through enhanced awareness of the many available financial optimizing techniques, enjoy great prosperity through the ages and for the benefit of our nation as a whole.

ALL BETS

In your youth, you had time to squander and invest, time to ignore the inevitable . . . death and estate taxes. But once you've reached 70 or 75, all bets are off. Death can come at any time and if you don't make plans to become financially prepared now, it's likely you'll never get the chance.

As I sat editing the final manuscript for this book, I received word that a good friend of mine had died. He was in his early 70's. He was a health and fitness nut . . . ate right, exercised, took care of himself. But his time had come. As will mine and as will yours. Any day, any hour, any moment. Ultimately, there is nothing we can do to stop it.

But, graced with the knowledge that the inevitable will occur, we

- **BUILD A 100 YEAR TAX FREE DYNASTY**

- **INCREASE CHARITABLE CONTRIBUTIONS UP TO 10 TIMES AT NO ADDITIONAL COST**

- **MULTIPLY ANNUAL TAX FREE GIFTS 100 TIMES**

- **AVOID FORCED LIQUIDATION**

- **BEAT ANY INVESTMENT WITH A 10 TO 1 RETURN**

ARE OFF!

can make plans to cheat death and estate taxes out of the ravages they would reap upon our loved ones. This book will tell you how.

ENJOY THE RICHES OF ESTATE PROTECTION THROUGHOUT YOUR LIFETIME

The best part about the Die Rich concepts presented in this book may well be the fact that they also let you live rich. Knowing that you will die rich, that your children will be financially secure and your loving legacy will continue intact, is the greatest wealth of all.

- **PROTECT YOUR HOME'S VALUE—PRESERVE IT FOR YOUR HEIRS**

- **$20 MILLION AT NO COST**

- **TURN $250 THOUSAND INTO $10 MILLION**

- **OPTIMIZE CAPITAL—$45 MILLION BECOMES $133 MILLION**

Contents

PART TWO
PROSPECT AND CLIENT EXAMPLES — 205

PART THREE
GLOSSARY — 257

Acknowledgements

IN ALL BOOKS of this type, there are numbers of people "behind the scenes" without whose personal caring, invaluable assistance and professional expertise the project would not be possible. This book is no exception.

Once again, there are not enough words to express my gratitude and appreciation to my contributing editor, Rhonda Morstein. This is the third book that she has contributed to and her ability to help organize my concepts and methods of communication are truly outstanding. She has become an insurance expert through our relationship and I am pleased and proud to have her associated with this project.

My thanks to Kristin Odermatt, Christine Slaughter and John Jacobson. Together they have created new designs in the graphics that appear throughout the book. They, too, have each developed a grasp of these complex and often difficult concepts in order to simplify the communication. Furthermore, special thanks to Kristin for her excellent graphic design on the two covers, front and back, of this book.

Once again, I am pleased to acknowledge Len Forman. He has indeed been a friend of long standing, a knowledgeable advisor, a consummate professional and, most important, a skilled publisher. This is our third book together and I really couldn't conceive of undertaking a project like this without his marvelous, able-bodied assistance.

Carl Waldman, an attorney in Los Angeles, has provided support material in regards to the Revocable Trust, Family Partnership and Home Grit, in addition to on-going legal advice and verification.

As usual, my most sincere thanks to my sons Alan Kaye and Howard Kaye and all of the Barry Kaye associates as well as our affiliated network of Wealth Creation Centers offices all over America. Their help, energy and follow-through with these concepts make it possible for the American public to realize the full benefits involved.

Foreword

I HAVE WRITTEN THIS BOOK as a follow-up to my recent book, *Save A Fortune On Your Estate Taxes*. The programs presented here elaborate on the information contained in that book and are tried and true concepts, many of which have been implemented with my own clientele, based on my thirty-two years of expertise within this specialized field. Die Rich goes much further and way beyond by introducing 52 concepts and ideas that I am now using and have used with my prospects and clients. These concepts can save and create millions and millions of dollars.

All the programs described in this book utilize life insurance as the investment means to secure the needed or desired return. *But this book is not about life insurance. If any other means were available to secure the same result, I would happily utilize it.* But there is not. As you will see on the following pages, no other investment vehicle accomplishes the guaranteed return life insurance produces for estate tax planning, wealth creation and preservation and for total money optimization.

In this book, I have chosen to concentrate on the ideas and concepts that can make or save a fortune for my readers rather than on the technical details of purchasing the actual policy(ies) or the legal ramifications of using these products. In this manner, you will have immediate access to information about the core concepts behind these money optimizing approaches.

Most of the methods described here will utilize one-pay, last-to-die policies to affect the greatest policy return, and to provide the greatest comparison with other investment vehicles. However *all policies can be financed and paid for over a period of any desired years.* Furthermore individual policies on males or females and combinations of whole life, blended whole life with term insurance, interest sensitive policies and universal life policies can all be used to accomplish the best individual results. Each individual situation must be analyzed to determine the best policy or combination of policies to achieve the most affective price and coverage. In all cases, I recommend a total diversification of your insurance portfolio in order to approach this subject from the most prudent and conservative basis.

All the figures quoted in the book are based on specific policies available at the time of its writing. There can or will be many changes based on the assumptions that prevail when your policy is purchased. Actual rates and premiums of the policies are based on current assumptions of mortality, interest and expense. Any changes from the current assumptions can increase or decrease the amount of premiums or length of time over which the same premium must be paid. Actual rates, explanations of existing policies at the time of your reading, or interest costs of implementation for any of the concepts discussed can be received by calling 1-800-DIE RICH (343-7424) and mentioning this book.

This book has been written primarily for people who have in excess of $1 million and who have "excess/surplus/discretionary" money that they can afford to transfer to their children, grandchildren or a trust in order to accomplish these concepts without impacting their current lifestyle. Some of the concepts can be utilized to buy an inheritance by people with less than $1 million in assets.

The true beauty of these concepts as they are used in estate planning is that they benefit everyone and harm no one. Your money is optimized, your children's financial security is protected, the U.S. government gets every dollar it has coming and the

American people benefit from increased funds available for investment. These are not "loopholes" that seek to avoid taxes and shortchange the government. These concepts let you live rich in the knowledge that you have done your best by yourself, your family and your country.

From the Publisher

THE AUTHOR DESCRIBES in this book many situations that he had available to him at the time. Without knowledge of your specific requirements, the author and publisher disclaim any liability for loss incurred by use of any direct or indirect application of the material contained herein. These ideas and concepts are only a starting point—only by using the proper professionals can you determine the complete suitability for your situation as well as consummate the proper implementation of these methods for optimizing and preserving your wealth for your family. Any change in the basic assumptions described herein will alter the specific results or returns. However, in most cases, the results will still be superior to those realized through any other approach. Naturally, all results are also limited by the assumed solvency of the company or consortium of companies which you elect to utilize.

Since any reference to an internal rate of return must be based on an assumed interest rate and period of time, there can be no such comparisons made, due to the uncertainty of when death will occur. In all cases, the author has diversified his client's portfolio and in most cases utilized less that 10% of the client's assets in doing so. Since he never proposes any course of financial action that would adversely affect his client's lifestyle, the internal rate of return is irrelevant in the context these ideas and concepts will provide.

You should consult your attorney for the implementation of any legal papers, such as trust documents, that may be necessary in carrying out these ideas. Trust officers can further provide you with the necessary information relative to these documents.

Some of the ideas and concepts in this book are based on many of the detailed explanations in Mr. Kaye's prior book, *Save A Fortune On Your Estate Taxes*. *Die Rich* could be considered the ultimate implementation, enhancement and consummation of the original material explained in the previous book. It is advisable that you secure a copy of that book if you wish to totally understand many of the basic foundations of the concepts and ideas contained herein.

A Message From Carole Kaye

FOR YEARS MY HUSBAND HAS SHARED with me the details of his concepts and I have watched as he has saved his clients billions of dollars in estate tax costs. But I have never been as excited by what can be accomplished as I am now.

The wealth creation and preservation techniques which culminate the more than 30 years he has worked in this field and which are presented in this book accomplish amazing things with money. They may sound too good to be true, yet they are true. They are like magic. And I know this, not only because I have read them but because I have seen them in action. Many of them are the same concepts which have allowed me to found and operate the largest contemporary museum of miniatures in the United States, The Carole and Barry Kaye Museum of Miniatures, and which will insure that my museum continues through my posterity. Many of them are the same methods which will insure the financial security of our children and allow them to follow their dreams.

Now, Barry is sharing, within the pages of this book, his knowledge and concepts with the American people. And I know that the same benefits which my family and I have reaped will be available to anyone with the foresight and ability to implement them.

It is another wonderful legacy for my family to know that Barry has created these revolutionary means for optimizing capital and protecting wealth. So many people will live happier, more secure lives as a result of his labor. So many people will see their dreams realized or preserved. And the savings which are generated and the wealth which is preserved will go on to benefit all America.

"Ma . . . Make Me Rich"

THIS IS THE THIRD BOOK of Barry Kaye's on which I have served as Contributing Editor. I was privileged to work with him on his two previous books, *Save A Fortune on Your Estate Taxes* and *Save A Fortune on Your Life Insurance.*

Each time a new book has come out, Mr. Kaye has given me several copies which I have distributed to family, friends and those of my acquaintance whom I thought could benefit from the wisdom contained within them. But as I worked with Mr. Kaye on the astonishing concepts contained within this book, I had a different plan in mind. During one of our editing sessions I told Mr. Kaye, "All I want when this book is done is one copy so I can send it to my mother with a note attached that says 'Ma . . . . make me rich! Here's how.' "

I love my mother very much and she knows that. If I could arrange things so that she could live forever, I certainly would. But we both know that someday she will die. I also know that she loves me very much and that she desires to carry on her living legacy of guidance and assistance—of parenting—even after she is gone. It makes her feel good to know she will have provided a better life for me and I know from personal experience that, while financial security does not prevent the hurt of losing a loved one, it can help avoid additional devastation.

My father worked hard to earn the legacy he left my mother. My mother has worked hard to preserve and enhance that legacy. Neither, I know, would wish to see it evaporate upon her death. Both would want it preserved and optimized.

So, while my somewhat flippant note will say, "Ma . . . make me rich" what it will really say is, "Mom . . . the means for you to best protect and express your loving gift to me are contained within these pages. I know how important it is to you to always be there helping me and that knowledge makes me love you even more."

Contributing Editor
Rhonda Morstein

How to Read This Book

THE CONCEPTS CONTAINED WITHIN THIS BOOK are sometimes of a highly technical nature that can be confusing to those not well versed in some of the legal terminology or financial maneuvering. We have tried to present the information in as clear and concise a manner as possible, but the nuances of estate tax planning and capital optimization do not easily lend themselves to brevity.

For this reason, we have included, following most sample concepts, graphics and charts which we believe greatly simplify the benefits of each plan. The graphics provide a visual representation of the process by which the result was realized. The charts detail the costs and savings of each plan at different estate levels and ages so that you can most easily apply the generalities of what you have read to your own situation. The charts also contrast the results of some programs with what will occur if the method is not employed.

Some of the charts have been broken down into estate levels of $3 million, $10 million and $50 million. We chose these numbers because they most easily allow you to customize the figures to your own estate value. The $3 million figures can easily become $30 million or $300 million by adding additional digits to all quoted figures across the board. $10 million can represent an estate of $1 million, $100 million, even $1 billion by adding or subtracting zeros as needed. Use the figures quoted in the $50 million example for estate values of $5 million or $500 million. Additionally, by simply dividing or multiplying the sums quoted in the $50 million column, you can easily see the amounts as they would apply to estates of $2.5 million, $25 million or $250 million.

In this same manner, the charts also depict insurance outlay at ages 60, 70 and 80. If your age falls somewhere between these ages, simply average the quotes based on your age differential.

In almost all cases, the examples given are based on the average age of a couple utilizing a last-to-die policy. Policies purchased on individuals rather than couples will have some variance in their results. For assistance in determining your costs, call 1-800-DIE-RICH (343-7424) and ask for rate assistance.

We recommend you read this book with a pencil and paper nearby to help you calculate the savings you can enjoy and the optimization you will realize when you apply these concepts to your own estate planning.

Introduction

DIE RICH, the title of this book, means exactly what it suggests: If you must die, you may as well do so leaving newly acquired or significantly optimized assets for your family. This book will show you how. Over 52 dramatic sample programs and client examples will take you through the process of creating and preserving great wealth for the posterity you must some day leave behind.

These ideas may seem incredible but each and every one is totally legal, relatively simple and guaranteed to provide a return far in excess of almost any other financial vehicle. They will optimize your money by reallocating your assets in such a way as to preserve all existing wealth or create substantially greater wealth. All the premises detailed are based, for the most part, on using relatively new, investment-oriented inheritance type policies from major, highly-rated life insurance companies. The leverage of life insurance combined with the tax advantages allowed by the government produce the best returns when compared with almost any investment, due to the certainty of eventual death.

Caspar Weinberger, Chairman of Forbes, conversing on the subject of financial planning, referred to many people engaged in estate planning as "Victims of Conventional Wisdom." His point was that, all too often, people fail to look beyond the accepted means of accomplishing a goal, and, in so doing, miss out on an even better way of achieving the same end.

Those words could not be more true then when applied to the uses of life insurance and irrevocable trusts as a means to create and preserve great wealth. Too often, people think of life insurance in archaic terms. They fail to recognize the outstanding opportunities it affords. They try to assess its value in terms of "internal rates of return" which have no bearing on the true leverage it provides and the guaranteed nature of its return. They are "Victims of Conventional Wisdom" and their inability to see beyond the accepted role of life insurance in family financial planning can cost them thousands, tens of thousands, hundreds of thousands and even millions of dollars.

Today's life insurance policies are not merely security against an "unforeseen death" as the conventional wisdom would suggest. How can death ever be unforeseen when eventually it must happen to us all? The new uses for insurance policies which are utilized throughout the concepts detailed in this book are investment vehicles predicated on the one guarantee which supersedes all others—the guarantee of death.

Some people try to base their life insurance needs on actuarial tables thinking they can plan accordingly or avoid acting because they have plenty of time left. They, too, are victims of conventional wisdom. But, as James J. Avery, Jr., FSA, Senior Vice President and Chief Operating Officer for Prudential has explained, *actuarial tables have absolutely no statistical value in individual planning.* Actuarial tables are valid only for large groups; the law of averages upon which they are based has no relevance for a single person or event. For example, the law of averages says that with each toss of a coin there is a fifty-fifty chance that it will come up either heads or tails. If you were to flip the coin 1,000 times, statistically you could expect about half of the flips to be heads. But a person doesn't get 1,000 chances at life to make it come out right. And there is every bit as much chance that your one flip will be tails. If heads is good fortune and tails is an early tragedy, there is no mathematical formula which can predict or insure which side your life will come up on.

You could also look at it in terms of the roll of a die (the pun, while not intended, is apt). Before it is thrown, each roll of the die has a one in six chance of coming up on a specific, chosen number. And, if the die is to be thrown enough times, statistical predictions can be made as to its expected behavior. But, once thrown the die is cast and, on a singular, individual basis, all the statistical probabilities under heaven will not affect its outcome.

Therein lies the truest expression of the value of life insurance. Because you can not know until you flip the coin or throw the dice what your result will be, there is no other investment vehicle available which protects the outcome like life insurance does.

Throughout the concepts detailed in this book, you will see uses of life insurance that far exceed the conventional wisdom. You will learn ways to use this increasingly valuable financial tool that produce highly optimized and guaranteed results regardless of whether your life comes up heads or tails.

Die Rich And Tax Free is divided into three basic parts.

Part One will show you over 40 concepts to preserve and optimize your current assets. Each idea is presented in simple, easy-to-understand terms in order to increase your comprehension. Accompanying each concept is a graphic explanation to further your understanding. Where applicable, there is an additional page which will show the conclusions outlined on the graphs based upon several initial variables including different age ranges, estate valuations and payment methods.

You will also learn some of the many additional benefits using life insurance to preserve your estate for your heirs provides. You will see how doing so is good for America, how it can dramatically help our charitable foundations and how using life insurance in these fashions truly becomes the ultimate gift you can give your loved ones.

Part Two actually depicts 12 cases of clients and prospects for whom some of these concepts have been implemented. From them, you should be able to make analogies to your own situation and imagine where the respective approaches may be applicable.

Part Three is an expanded glossary of insurance and legal terms meant to simply define the sometimes confusing legal and insurance industry terms used in discussions of policies and trusts.

Every concept, plan and method utilized in the examples within these pages is accurate, true and legal under current assumptions. And every one will move you much, much closer to the goal of dying—and living—rich.

Part One

❦

SAMPLE PROGRAMS

THERE IS A CURRENT ASSUMPTION that the wealthy do not pay their "fair share" of taxes, that the middle class bears a disproportionate tax burden. We know that assumption to be completely false. In fact, the rich pay huge taxes. Estate taxes alone can claim from 37% to 60% of an estate valued at $3 million or more. This means that if you have amassed $3 million, your estate taxes will be $1.1 million—leaving your immediate, first-generation heirs only $1.9 million. If your estate is worth $10 million, your taxes are $4.8 million leaving only $5.2 million. If your estate is worth $50 million, estate taxes will take $27.5 million; your immediate heirs will inherit $22.5 million, less than half your original worth.

In his 1993 *Forbes 400* magazine article, Dave Dreman made this remarkable observation: "For those of you who don't have much capital but dream of one day getting on The Forbes Four Hundred List, I have bad news: The odds against you are about 650,000 to 1. *For those who dream of establishing a family dynasty and passing great wealth on to your descendants, the odds of making the FORBES list and staying on it for four generations are close to 1 in 500 million.*

"In short," Mr. Dreman continues, "the odds against a family staying rich are many times greater than the odds of getting rich.

For those who dream only of modest wealth, the odds are not much better for passing it on to your heirs. *It is easier to make money than it is to keep money* . . . In real life riches to rags is as common as rags to riches."

But there is a way to not only preserve the wealth you already enjoy but to also increase that wealth manyfold, reducing or avoiding, along the way, the financial devastation of estate taxes. And you will learn how on the pages to come. The following sample programs will teach you how to use the guaranteed return of life insurance (guaranteed because of the guaranteed nature of death). However all returns are based on current assumptions and subject to the solvency of the insurance company providing the benefits to create miracles of financial growth and retention.

There is no other financial vehicle—no stock, bond, annuity, mutual fund, retirement or pension plan—*that can guarantee to create and preserve wealth as these plans will.* There is no investment strategy or program that can match the *guaranteed* power these plans have to maintain and increase the assets you've amassed. These are not merely ideas or speculations—they are absolutely irrefutable, legal and proven programs which will reap *guaranteed* results.

As you read each of the following sample concepts, customize them for your own situation to see how dramatic your own savings and optimization can be. The easiest way to accomplish this is to add or subtract digits (i.e. if $10 million is used as an example, subtract a digit to make it $1 million or add a digit to make it $100 million, whichever is nearest to your estate value; if $50 million is used, add or subtract digits to make it $5 million or $500 million) to reach a closer approximation of your own situation. In this way, you will transcend the theoretical concepts to more fully understand the full personal value each program offers.

❦ Preserve Your Wealth

This book has been conceived primarily to share the knowledge and conviction that you can greatly reduce or totally eliminate all estate taxes. Each of the concepts presented uses as its basis one simple plan and method from which all the others evolve. To understand the concepts which will be presented on the following pages, you must first understand this underlying program.

If you're 70 years old and have worked hard for fifty years amassing a significant estate for the intended benefit of your children and grandchildren, you may be dismayed to discover that, in reality, you spent 27 of those years working solely for the benefit of one relative—your Uncle Sam. Estate taxes will take 55% of your total assets, 27 years worth of your sweat equity. Your family will receive the benefit of only 23 years of your labor.

Assuming that the estate you've built is worth $30 million, estate taxes will consume $16.5 million. Your heirs will be left with $13.5 million to be divided among them. If you have three children to whom you are leaving your estate, each will receive only $4.5 million as opposed to the $10 million each you thought you had worked to provide them. At current interest rates of approximately 5%, that means each child will have yearly income earnings of $225 thousand, less than half of the $500 thousand their $10 million would have produced.

By the time your heirs pass the $16.5 million of their combined inheritance along to their heirs, estate taxes will have reduced it to $7.43 million.

There is one way, and one way only, guaranteed to stop the decimation of your assets by estate taxation. One way, and one way only, guaranteed to help preserve your wealth intact for the benefit of your loved ones.

If you were to transfer $3.3 million to an irrevocable trust, that trust could purchase a one-pay, last-to-die insurance policy which, at an average age of 70 for a husband and wife, would yield a 5-times return of $16.5 million, based on current assumptions. Because the policy was purchased through an irrevocable trust, a legal entity separate from your estate, your heirs would receive the $16.5 million benefit *income and estate tax free*. The government would still take $16.5 million in estate taxes, but the insurance proceeds would *replace it completely* and your beneficiaries would inherit the full $30 million you had amassed.

The cost of such a plan is negligible in comparison to the cost of estate taxes. Since both you and your spouse are allowed a $600 thousand Unified Estate and Gift Tax Credit, the first $1.2 million of the money transferred to the irrevocable trust would be a tax exempt gift. The remaining $2.1 million would be taxable at an average rate of 50%. But even so, $1 million in gift taxes is a far cry from $16.5 million in estate taxes even when added to $3.3 million of insurance premium.

Of course, the plan only works if you do not need the $3.3 million of insurance premium cost and $1 million of gift tax cost to sustain your lifestyle. Or, more accurately, if you do not need the $215 thousand that the combined $4.3 million produces in yearly income. With an estate of $30 million, you will still be left with $25.7 million in principal possibly producing $1.2 million per year. If that is enough to ensure that you and your spouse can maintain the lifestyle you have earned and become accustomed to, then the one time expense of $1 million in gift taxes—though the only real cost is the $50 thousand per year interest income this $1 million would earn—and the yearly loss of $215 thousand in discretionary interest income could not be better spent.

Through this simple, affordable and completely legal plan, your estate is preserved intact for your heirs and your estate tax cost is effectively reduced by 74%, from $16.5 million to $4.3 million.

Different average ages, marital and health status, estate valuations, and methods of insurance policy payment, will alter the specific financial outcome for this plan or any of the others detailed on the following pages. If your average age was 60 and you had the same $30 million estate, the cost of an insurance policy to replace the $16.5 million estate taxes would be $1.65 million and you would reduce your estate tax costs by 90%. If your average age was 80, the cost would be $5.5 million—still a 67% reduction.

Using this plan as a basic concept, the coming pages will detail forty ways of preserving and creating great wealth for your family throughout the generations to come. They will show you how to bequeath generous gifts to your favorite charity without any impact to your family's financial security, how to recover losses on real estate or stock transactions at virtually no cost, how to create a perpetual dynasty of wealth for your children, grandchildren and great-grandchildren, how to double your gross estate and triple your net estate.

You may find it difficult to believe that a plan so simple can really work. You may wonder if it is indeed too good to be true. But every method presented here is completely legal, tax free and doable. *There are no ifs, ands or buts.* There are no legal provisos. These plans are every bit as uncomplicated as they seem. And they work. Guaranteed.

1M at 5% = 50,000

4.3m al 5% = 215,000

1

Die Rich and Tax Free

OFTENTIMES, when people get to the age where they are contemplating how to assign their assets, they are torn between wanting to leave their children as financially secure as possible and wanting to give something back to the community in the form of a significant charitable donation. While our children usually come first in our affections, there is a special joy in knowing that some university, hospital, foundation or cause of our choosing will benefit from our generosity.

If you were told that such a difficult decision was unnecessary, that, in fact, you could virtually double your net assets and eliminate all estate tax costs so that both your children and selected charity could receive the full value of your estate, wouldn't you want to take advantage of that fact? Well, you can.

Under "normal" circumstances, if you have an estate worth $10 million, estate taxes would cost approximately $5 million. This would leave only $5 million. But there is a way in which *you can leave your heirs and your favorite charity more than the full $10 million at no additional cost to you!*

Assuming that you and your spouse enjoy an average age of 60, you could transfer $1 million to an irrevocable trust for your children. You would pay no gift taxes in doing so since under current law you and your spouse can transfer $1.2 million gift tax free. If you have already used your Unified Estate and Gift Tax

Credit (exemption), you would either pay a small gift tax or you could transfer the money over a period of years using your annual $10 thousand exclusions.

The trust would purchase a one-payment, last-to-die insurance policy which, based on current assumptions, would pay your heirs $10 million upon your deaths which they would receive income and estate tax free. Your children would inherit the full $10 million of your amassed wealth free from the decimation of estate taxation.

At your deaths, you would transfer all your remaining money (your total assets) to your favorite charity or charities. Since charitable donations are tax deductible, you would, in effect, eliminate all estate taxes. In this way, your favorite charity(ies) will receive $9 million, the original value of your $10 million estate less the $1 million you transferred to the trust to purchase for your family the insurance policy, estate and income tax free.

You would have virtually doubled your net worth and left both your children and chosen charity more than the entire original value of your estate without having paid any estate taxes!

You could even enhance the potential of this program. Instead of leaving your assets to any specific charity or charities, you could use them to create your own charitable foundation and endow it with $9 million. This would accomplish the same goal of charitable contribution and, in addition, would produce an on-going mechanism for your children and/or other family members to receive income as trustee(s) of the foundation. The foundation could exist virtually in perpetuity using the income the $9 million produces to do good works for the community or cause you select.

Of course, as with all our methods, this plan should not be undertaken if you need the money you will transfer to the irrevocable trust in order to support your lifestyle. Keep in mind that you will still have $9 million to provide for your needs. And also remember that the true cost to you of this plan is not $1 million— in all likelihood you would never have spent the principal—it is only the $50 thousand in projected yearly income interest, assuming a 5% rate of return. If you have $50 thousand a year in discretionary income, can you think of a greater or more satisfying use to which you could put it than to insure the full financial well-being of your children while, at the same time, creating a generous legacy of charitable endowment?

Think of it ... $50 thousand a year in surplus, discretionary money guarantees $10 million tax free to your children; $9 million to your favorite charity—$450 thousand per year (based on current interest assumptions of 5%) in perpetuity—while your children receive yearly income for their work on behalf of your charitable foundation for the rest of their lives allowing you to truly *die rich and tax free.*

50% GOES TO YOUR FAMILY
OR
190% GOES TO YOUR HEIRS & CHARITY

CURRENT METHOD

| Estate Value $10 Million | → At Death → | Estate Taxes $5 Million | → | Heirs Receive $5 Million |

DIE RICH METHOD

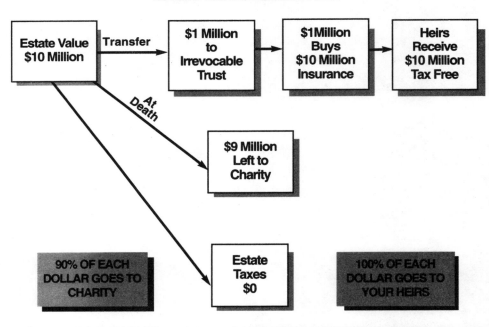

DIE RICH AND TAX FREE

All figures are based on current assumptions. Charts are for illustrative purposes only.
This illustration used a last-to-die insurance policy for a male and female both age 60.
©1994 WEALTH CREATION CENTERS℠ - Barry Kaye Associates

DIE RICH & Tax Free

$3,000,000 ESTATE	Current	AGE 60		AGE 70		AGE 80	
		1 Pay	7 Pay	1 Pay	7 Pay	1 Pay	7 Pay
Estate Value	$3,000,000	$3,000,000	$3,000,000	$3,000,000	$3,000,000	$3,000,000	$3,000,000
Buy Insurance	$0	$3,000,000	$3,000,000	$3,000,000	$3,000,000	$3,000,000	$3,000,000
Cost of Ins.	$0	($386,555)	($65,502)	($621,295)	($106,454)	($882,684)	($157,220)
Net Estate	$0	$2,613,445	$2,541,486	$2,378,705	$2,254,822	$2,117,316	$1,899,460
Estate Taxes	($1,100,000)	$0	$0	$0	$0	$0	$0
Gift Tax	$0	$0	$0	$0	$0	$0	$0
Net to Charity	$0	$2,613,445	$2,541,486	$2,378,705	$2,254,822	$2,117,316	$1,899,460
Net to Family	$1,900,000	$3,000,000	$3,000,000	$3,000,000	$3,000,000	$3,000,000	$3,000,000

$10,000,000 ESTATE	Current	AGE 60		AGE 70		AGE 80	
		1 Pay	7 Pay	1 Pay	7 Pay	1 Pay	7 Pay
Estate Value	$10,000,000	$10,000,000	$10,000,000	$10,000,000	$10,000,000	$10,000,000	$10,000,000
Buy Insurance	$0	$10,000,000	$10,000,000	$10,000,000	$10,000,000	$10,000,000	$10,000,000
Cost of Ins.	$0	($1,286,862)	($218,057)	($2,069,537)	($354,598)	($2,941,140)	($523,867)
Net Estate	$0	$8,713,138	$8,473,601	$7,930,463	$7,517,814	$7,058,860	$6,332,931
Estate Taxes	($5,000,000)	$0	$0	$0	$0	$0	$0
Gift Tax	$0	$0	$0	$0	$0	$0	$0
Net to Charity	$0	$8,713,138	$8,473,601	$7,930,463	$7,517,814	$7,058,860	$6,332,931
Net to Family	$5,000,000	$10,000,000	$10,000,000	$10,000,000	$10,000,000	$10,000,000	$10,000,000

$50,000,000 ESTATE	Current	AGE 60		AGE 70		AGE 80	
		1 Pay	7 Pay	1 Pay	7 Pay	1 Pay	7 Pay
Estate Value	$50,000,000	$50,000,000	$50,000,000	$50,000,000	$50,000,000	$50,000,000	$50,000,000
Buy Insurance	$0	$50,000,000	$50,000,000	$50,000,000	$50,000,000	$50,000,000	$50,000,000
Cost of Ins.	$0	($6,431,474)	($1,089,802)	($10,345,213)	($1,772,563)	($14,703,744)	($2,618,988)
Net Estate	$0	$43,568,526	$42,371,386	$39,654,787	$37,592,059	$35,296,256	$31,667,084
Estate Taxes	($27,500,000)	$0	$0	$0	$0	$0	$0
Gift Tax	$0	($3,215,737)	($3,814,307)	($5,172,607)	($6,203,971)	($7,351,872)	($9,166,458)
Net to Charity	$0	$40,352,789	$38,557,079	$34,482,180	$31,388,088	$27,944,384	$22,500,626
Net to Family	$22,500,000	$50,000,000	$50,000,000	$50,000,000	$50,000,000	$50,000,000	$50,000,000

All figures are based on current assumptions. Charts are for illustrative purposes only.
©1994 WEALTH CREATION CENTERS℠ - Barry Kaye Associates

2

Borrow $5 Million at 1/2% Interest— $25 Thousand—Per Year

How did you buy your house? Did you pay cash for it or did you finance it with a mortgage?

How did you build your business? Did you only work with the resources in hand or did you borrow against receivables, finance equipment purchases, take out loans and lines of credit?

In all likelihood, the answer is that you took advantage of available financing to optimize your financial potential. It's the smart, accepted way to do things. Yet, even if you are used to thinking in terms of financing for the purchase of a home, the lease of a car, the funding of a business, chances are you're still stuck thinking about paying estate taxes in one lump sum due in total nine months after your death. Even if you are familiar with the basics of using life insurance proceeds to significantly discount estate tax costs, you probably limit your thinking to the purchasing of policies from income or with principal transferred from your estate.

But why? Why wouldn't you apply the same elementary concepts of financing major purchases or expansions to financing one of the single largest expenditures your estate will ever need to make: the up to 55% of its total value which will be due in estate taxes nine months after your death? If you really care about protecting your heirs from estate tax devastation, why haven't you built the cost of insurance funding to recover the estate tax cost into your budget? *Particularly when you can do so for an effective ½ % yearly—less than 1%!—of the needed amount without losing or transferring a single dollar of interest-producing principal or income during your lifetime!*

Consider this: you have an estate worth $10 million. You *know* you are going to die, it's unavoidable. You *know* that, at your death, $5 million of your estate *must* be paid in estate taxes. And you *know* that, unless you take some action to prevent it, your heirs will be left with only half your original estate value.

If you and your spouse are average age 60, you could purchase a one-pay, last-to-die insurance policy which would pay a death benefit of $5 million to replace the estate tax costs for your heirs, for only $500 thousand, based on current assumptions. Transferred to an irrevocable trust, that $500 thousand produces $5 million which will come to your heirs income and estate tax free. Though the government will take $5 million, the insurance will replace it and your heirs will inherit the full $10 million you had intended for them.

But you need not use principal or income to make the insurance purchase. With an estate of $10 million, you can easily borrow the $500 thousand. At 5% interest, the loan would cost you $25 thousand per year. *So the $25 thousand yearly interest effectively borrows $5 million!* Forget about the middle steps—forget about the fact that the $25 thousand is actually paying interest on a $500 thousand loan which is being used to purchase the $5 million in life insurance. It really doesn't matter. *The only thing which really counts is that the $25 thousand yearly loan payments are funding an ultimate return of $5 million—and that's a ½ % interest effective loan cost.* One-half of one-percent yearly recovers the full $5 million of estate tax costs. At those rates, who could afford not to?

Even better, for an additional .1%, you can recover the cost of the $500 thousand loan itself!

At the same average age of 60, using the same one-pay, last-to-die insurance policy, the cost to provide an additional $500 thousand in excess of the $5 million needed to recover the estate tax costs would cost $50 thousand, based on current assumptions. Now you are purchasing $5.5 million in death benefit for $550 thousand. And the interest cost on the $550 thousand loan is $27.5 thousand which is still effectively .5%. But, in fairness, you're not really getting $5.5 million, you're getting $5 million—the additional $500 thousand is repaying the principal loan amount. So you're heirs will really only receive the same $5 million but without a $500 thousand outstanding loan balance to be repaid. *That means you've financed $5 million at a yearly cost of $27.5 thousand and that's about .06%.*

Even at older ages, the costs are minuscule in comparison with the return.

At average age 70, a last-to-die policy with a $5 million death benefit would cost $1 million, based on current assumptions. Financing the $1 million would cost $50 thousand a year assuming 5% interest. That makes the effective rate for producing the needed $5 million, only 1%. To recover the borrowed $1 million would require an additional $200 thousand in premiums which would add $10 thousand a year to the overall loan repayments making them $60 thousand. This would raise the yearly interest to 1.2% to recover in full the $5 million in estate tax costs.

At average age 80, the $5 million insurance policy would cost $1.6 million based on current assumptions which, if borrowed, would cost $85 thousand a year providing, effectively, $5 million for 1.7% interest. It would then take an additional $533 thousand to buy enough insurance to recover the original $1.6 million raising the total loan to $2.1 million which would cost $105 thousand per year. So, in effect, the $5 million tax cost would be recovered in full for a loan of $2.1 million at approximately 2.2%.

If it is your desire to take the eventual and unavoidable costs of estate taxes into your overall financial planning, there is no more effective and optimized way to do so then to recoup the entire costs for your heirs at the insignificant rates of .6% to 2.2% effectively. Your estate will almost assuredly face no costs as massive as estate taxes and can fund no financial return at rates more affordable.

BORROW $5 MILLION FOR $25,000 INTEREST A YEAR

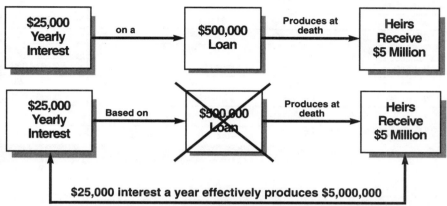

| $25,000 Yearly Interest | on a | $500,000 Loan | Produces at death | Heirs Receive $5 Million |

| $25,000 Yearly Interest | Based on | $500,000 Loan | Produces at death | Heirs Receive $5 Million |

$25,000 interest a year effectively produces $5,000,000

For all practical purposes you borrowed $5,000,000 but only pay $25,000 per year in interest.

$500,000 LOAN PAYBACK ONLY $250,000

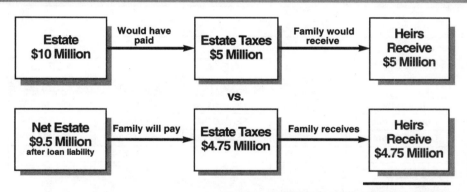

| Estate $10 Million | Would have paid | Estate Taxes $5 Million | Family would receive | Heirs Receive $5 Million |

vs.

| Net Estate $9.5 Million after loan liability | Family will pay | Estate Taxes $4.75 Million | Family receives | Heirs Receive $4.75 Million |

NET COST OF LOAN = $250,000

EFFECTIVELY UNCLE SAM PAYS OFF 50% OF YOUR LOAN AT YOUR DEATH

All figures are based on current assumptions. Charts are for illustrative purposes only.
This illustration used a last-to-die insurance policy for a male and female both age 60.
©1994 WEALTH CREATION CENTERS℠ - Barry Kaye Associates

$3,000,000 ESTATE

	Current	AGE 60 1 Pay	AGE 70 1 Pay	AGE 80 1 Pay
Estate Value	$3,000,000	$3,000,000	$3,000,000	$3,000,000
Buy Insurance	$0	$1,100,000	($1,100,000)	($1,100,000)
Cost of Insurance	$0	($142,187)	($228,200)	($323,961)
Loan Amount	$0	$142,187	$228,200	$323,961
Gift Tax	$0	$0	$0	$0
Yearly Interest	$0	($7,109)	($11,410)	($16,198)
Net Estate	$0	$2,857,813	$2,771,800	$2,676,039
Estate Tax	($1,100,000)	$0	$0	$0
Net to Family	$1,900,000	$2,928,907	$2,885,900	$2,838,020

$10,000,000 ESTATE

	Current	AGE 60 1 Pay	AGE 70 1 Pay	AGE 80 1 Pay
Estate Value	$10,000,000	$10,000,000	$10,000,000	$10,000,000
Buy Insurance	$0	$5,000,000	$5,000,000	$5,000,000
Cost of Insurance	$0	($643,786)	($1,035,078)	($1,470,815)
Loan Amount	$0	$643,786	$1,035,078	$1,470,815
Gift Tax	$0	$0	$0	$0
Yearly Interest	$0	($32,189)	($51,754)	($73,541)
Net Estate	$0	$9,356,214	$8,964,922	$8,529,185
Estate Tax	($5,000,000)	$0	$0	$0
Net to Family	$5,000,000	$9,678,107	$9,482,461	$9,264,593

$50,000,000 ESTATE

	Current	AGE 60 1 Pay	AGE 70 1 Pay	AGE 80 1 Pay
Estate Value	$50,000,000	$50,000,000	$50,000,000	$50,000,000
Buy Insurance	$0	$27,500,000	$27,500,000	$27,500,000
Cost of Insurance	$0	($3,537,628)	($5,690,143)	($8,087,279)
Loan Amount	$0	$3,537,628	$5,690,143	$8,087,279
Gift Tax	$0	($1,768,814)	($2,845,072)	($4,043,640)
Yearly Interest	$0	($265,322)	($426,761)	($606,546)
Net Estate	$0	$44,693,558	$41,464,785	$37,869,081
Estate Tax	($27,500,000)	$0	$0	$0
Net to Family	$22,500,000	$46,462,372	$44,309,857	$41,912,721

All figures are based on current assumptions. Charts are for illustrative purposes only.
©1994 WEALTH CREATION CENTERS℠ - Barry Kaye Associates

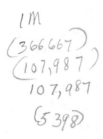

3

Borrow Away Your Tax—
Buy $10 Million for
$100 Thousand a Year

WHY WOULD YOU ALLOW your stock portfolio to be devalued up to 55% by estate taxes when you could retain its entire worth for a fraction of the cost?

Your stock portfolio can provide the leverage to protect its own entire worth. Using the margin available through your principal assets, you can borrow the funds to purchase enough life insurance to pay the estate taxes which will be due upon the assets at your death.

A 70 year old man has a stock portfolio worth $19 million. Estate taxes will devalue the principal by about $10 million. He could sell $2 million worth of the stock and, at a 5–1 return, purchase $10 million in insurance to pay the estate taxes, but he doesn't want to pay the capital gains taxes on the profit he earns. He also enjoys playing the market and doesn't want to give up the funds with which he indulges his pleasure. Furthermore, he derives a feeling of safety knowing the principal is there for him in case of financial emergency.

Using the borrowing power inherent in his portfolio, he can protect the entire $19 million for $100 thousand per year without having to sell a single share.

Using the margin available through his stock brokerage firm, the man borrows $2 million against his portfolio, transfers it to an irrevocable trust which uses it to purchase a $10 million last-to-die insurance policy. Upon his and his wife's deaths, their heirs will receive the full $10 million, tax free, to offset the $10 million in estate taxes that will be levied against his $19 million estate.

At current broker's call rates of 5%, the $2 million loan will cost only $100 thousand in interest per year making the effective cost of his $10 million coverage $100 thousand per year—a 100–1 return at the beginning!

At death, the man's heirs will have to repay the $2 million loan principal. While this will reduce their full $19 million inheritance to $17 million, it is still $8 million more than it would have been had he not purchased the insurance to replace the estate taxes. *It would take 80 years of paying $100 thousand interest on the $2 million loan to equal this $8 million.* But the man and his wife are 70 years old. Facing reality, perhaps they have 10, maybe 20, years left to live. If so, the loan cost will be between $1 million and $2 million. So now his heirs have "lost" $1 million or so more—though this $1 million would not have existed if the man hadn't margined his portfolio. Even so, this still reduces their inheritance to 'only' $16 million—$7 million more than they would have received otherwise. And there is always the possibility that the couple will not live another ten years. In the unfortunate circumstance that they die after one year, their heirs will receive the whole $10 million insurance for a cost of only one $100 thousand payment.

And, of course, as you saw in the preceding example, it is also possible to borrow enough to fund the purchase of enough insurance to not only recover the full estate tax but to cover the cost of the initial loan amount as well.

If the couple were 60 at the time the man margined his stocks, loan payments might have to be made for a longer time period. With the same 81-year life expectancy, payments would be made for 21 years totalling $2.1 million—if the same $2 million were borrowed. But, since the return on the insurance investment is twice as great at 60 as it is at 70, he would only need to margin $1 million worth of stock in order to purchase enough insurance to earn the same $10 million return. The yearly payments on the $1 million loan would be only $50 thousand which, over 21 years, would equal $1 million—virtually the same cost as 10 yearly $100 thousand payments on a $2 million loan. And the couple still receives the same guaranteed insurance pay off if they only live 1 year, 10 years or 30 years.

By leveraging his stock portfolio, the man holds all his stocks, avoids paying any capital gains tax and still purchases the insurance needed to retain their full value for his heirs.

There is no way your children will be able to borrow enough against what remains of your estate after 50%–55% has been lost to estate taxes to ever recover its full value. But you can easily and affordably borrow against your current estate's value ample funds for them to recover the entire estate tax cost. So why wouldn't you?

BORROW AWAY YOUR TAX

	CURRENT METHOD	DIE RICH METHOD	DIE RICH+ METHOD
Gross Estate	$19,000,000	$19,000,000	$19,000,000
Sell Stock	$0	$3,000,000	$0
Borrow $2 Million for $100,000 Yearly	$0	$0	$2,000,000
Capital Gains Tax	$0	($1,000,000)	$0
Buys $10 Million Insurance	$0	($2,000,000)	($2,000,000)
Estate Tax	($10,450,000)	($8,800,000)	($9,300,000)
Insurance Pays	$0	$10,000,000	$10,000,000
Net Estate	$8,550,000	$17,200,000	$17,650,000

Avoid Capital Gains Tax

Retain Your Stock Portfolio

Increase Net Estate By $450,000

BUY $10 MILLION FOR $100,000 YEARLY

All figures are based on current assumptions. Charts are for illustrative purposes only.
This illustration used a last-to-die insurance policy for a male and female both age 70.
©1994 WEALTH CREATION CENTERS℠ - Barry Kaye Associates

4

Optimization of Assets— turn $100 Thousand a Year Into $86 Million

THIS CONCEPT IS, without question, the ultimate expression of everything which the methods you will learn in this book can accomplish. It uses numerous planning mechanisms in various combinations to optimize assets and produce returns beyond anything before imagined.

Sounds too good to be true? Sounds impossible? Well, it's neither. This program is absolutely true, simple and legal and it will, based on current assumptions, produce the exact results demonstrated. Here's how:

For the sake of this demonstration, assume you have a $10 million stock/bond portfolio. (To translate the numbers into your own situation, simply add or subtract a digit where applicable.) Obviously, having that significant an account, your broker will gladly margin $2 million at call rates—currently approximately 5%. You borrow the $2 million at a cost of $100 thousand per year.

In truth, you would not necessarily even have to pay this $100 thousand interest yearly. With an account of $10 million, your broker will have no objection to allowing the loan interest to accrue. At death, when the account is transferred to your heirs, they will receive the $10 million less the $2 million loan less the accrued unpaid interest. However, they will recover these costs, plus a significant additional amount, through the return on the insurance this plan will produce. Nonetheless, for the sake of this example, assume you pay the yearly $100 thousand in interest. With a $10 million portfolio it is fair to assume that you can afford the loan payments and, if so, you might as well make the payments. The return you receive will be more than worth it.

Now you have $2 million which you borrowed against your stocks. You gift it to charity with the instructions that $1 million be dedicated to funding current operations. The second $1 million is set aside for a future endowment and, in fact, is used by the charity to purchase a last-to-die insurance policy on the lives of you and your spouse. If you are age 60, that policy will produce an additional $10 million for the charity, based on current assumptions. If you are age 70, it will produce $5 million and if you are age 80 it will produce $3 million. The charity receives not the $2 million of your original gift but a total of $4 million (age 80) to $11 million (age 60).

You might think that this return was benefit enough . . . that turning $100 thousand a year, which it is possible you need not actually pay, into $11 million for charity was sufficient. But there is even more which that same annual $100 thousand can do— remember, you still want your children to recover the cost of your generous charitable donation.

The $2 million charitable donation is fully tax deductible. Assuming you are in a combined state and federal 50% income tax bracket (which, given your $10 million portfolio, is a fair assumption to make), that means you will realize a $1 million tax savings in the very first year—$1 million in taxes you will not have to pay. *Where else could you receive a $1 million tax credit for $100 thousand?* (Deductions are based on your adjusted gross income and can be carried over a 5 year period. Your accountant must be consulted to verify your deductibility.)

Using that saved $1 million, you purchase a life insurance policy on behalf of your children. Again, based on current assumptions, they will receive $10 million if you and your spouse are average age 60, $5 million if you are average age 70 and $3 million if you are average age 80. *Your annual $100 thousand has now grossed up to $21 million*—$11 million for charity and $10 million for your children if you are average age 60.

The actual cost of performing this amazing feat of financial leveraging is only $1 million. Your original estate was worth $10 million and would have been subject to $5 million in estate taxes leaving only $5 million for your heirs. After transferring the $2 million to charity your estate was decreased to $8 million on which $4 million of estate taxes will be levied leaving your heirs $4 million at your deaths. The difference of $1 million is the effective total cost of the program. You might say that Uncle Sam had paid back half of your $2 million loan for you.

But there's more—you can optimize this program even further.

If you took the $1 million in tax savings and used it to purchase insurance on your children for the sake of your grandchildren, it could earn a 40–50 times return for their benefit. *In this way the $1 million would produce $40–$50 million which, in addition to the $11 million going to charity, means your yearly $100 thousand interest produces $51 million to $61 million!*

There are many other ways in which this plan could be implemented for the greater benefit of your children or charity. You could take the $1 million tax savings and use it to purchase additional insurance for the charity earning up to an additional 10 times return if you purchase the policy on yourself and your wife (age 60) or up to an additional 50 times return if you purchase it on your children (age 40). Then, the charity would receive $1 million now for current operating expenses, $10 million at your death and an additional $50 million at the death of your child! The charity would receive a total of $61 million, all from the $100 thousand interest per year which you pay on the $2 million loan.

But keep in mind, you would now have donated your original

$1 million tax savings to charity and would earn another $500 thousand in tax savings. You could use that money to purchase insurance on you for your children—producing up to $5 million, based on current assumptions—or on your children on behalf of their children—thereby producing up to $25 million. *In this manner, your $100 thousand yearly produces up to $61 million for the charity and up to $25 million for your grandchildren—a total of $86 million!*

$7 - $21 MILLION FOR YOUR HEIRS, CHARITY & FOUNDATION FOR $100,000

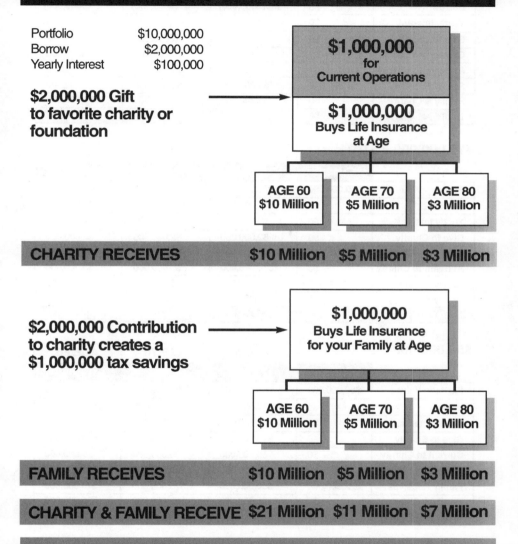

Portfolio $10,000,000
Borrow $2,000,000
Yearly Interest $100,000

$2,000,000 Gift to favorite charity or foundation

$1,000,000 for Current Operations

$1,000,000 Buys Life Insurance at Age

| AGE 60 | AGE 70 | AGE 80 |
| $10 Million | $5 Million | $3 Million |

CHARITY RECEIVES $10 Million $5 Million $3 Million

$2,000,000 Contribution to charity creates a $1,000,000 tax savings

$1,000,000 Buys Life Insurance for your Family at Age

| AGE 60 | AGE 70 | AGE 80 |
| $10 Million | $5 Million | $3 Million |

FAMILY RECEIVES $10 Million $5 Million $3 Million

CHARITY & FAMILY RECEIVE $21 Million $11 Million $7 Million

ALL FOR $100,000 A YEAR INTEREST!

Add or remove a zero for larger or smaller estates.

All figures are based on current assumptions. Charts are for illustrative purposes only.

©1994 WEALTH CREATION CENTERS℠ - Barry Kaye Associates

$3,000,000 ESTATE

	Current	AGE 60 1 Pay	AGE 70 1 Pay	AGE 80 1 Pay
Portfolio Value	$3,000,000	$3,000,000	$3,000,000	$3,000,000
Borrow	$0	($600,000)	($600,000)	($600,000)
Yearly Interest	$0	($30,000)	($30,000)	($30,000)
Give to Charity	$0	$600,000	$600,000	$600,000
Current to Charity	$0	$300,000	$300,000	$300,000
At Death to Charity	$0	$3,000,000	$1,500,000	$900,000
Family Receives	$1,900,000	$3,000,000	$1,500,000	$900,000
Family & Charity	$0	$6,300,000	$3,300,000	$2,100,000
Total Cost Yearly	$0	($30,000)	($30,000)	($30,000)

$10,000,000 ESTATE

	Current	AGE 60 1 Pay	AGE 70 1 Pay	AGE 80 1 Pay
Portfolio Value	$10,000,000	$10,000,000	$10,000,000	$10,000,000
Borrow	$0	($2,000,000)	($2,000,000)	($2,000,000)
Yearly Interest	$0	($100,000)	($100,000)	($100,000)
Give to Charity	$0	$2,000,000	$2,000,000	$2,000,000
Current to Charity	$0	$1,000,000	$1,000,000	$1,000,000
At Death to Charity	$0	$10,000,000	$5,000,000	$3,000,000
Family Receives	$5,000,000	$10,000,000	$5,000,000	$3,000,000
Family & Charity	$0	$21,000,000	$11,000,000	$7,000,000
Total Cost Yearly	$0	($100,000)	($100,000)	($100,000)

$50,000,000 ESTATE

	Current	AGE 60 1 Pay	AGE 70 1 Pay	AGE 80 1 Pay
Portfolio Value	$50,000,000	$50,000,000	$50,000,000	$50,000,000
Borrow	$0	($10,000,000)	($10,000,000)	($10,000,000)
Yearly Interest	$0	($500,000)	($500,000)	($500,000)
Give to Charity	$0	$10,000,000	$10,000,000	$10,000,000
Current to Charity	$0	$5,000,000	$5,000,000	$5,000,000
At Death to Charity	$0	$50,000,000	$25,000,000	$15,000,000
Family Receives	$22,500,000	$50,000,000	$25,000,000	$15,000,000
Family & Charity	$0	$105,000,000	$55,000,000	$35,000,000
Total Cost Yearly	$0	($500,000)	($500,000)	($500,000)

All figures are based on current assumptions. Charts are for illustrative purposes only.
©1994 WEALTH CREATION CENTERS℠ - Barry Kaye Associates

5

==

Estate Tax Cost Discount—
Turn $5 Million Into $10 Million

When you die, and you will, the government will take up to 55% of all you have amassed and leave your heirs only 45%. You can protest, "It's not fair!", you can be outraged, you can try and earn as much as possible to still have a considerable amount left for your children after these ravages are assessed. But you cannot live forever and your family must pay the taxes the government claims. Death and taxes—still the only two things of which you can be sure.

But there is no finite law which says you cannot eliminate or greatly reduce the cost of that tax loss. Nothing which prevents you from replacing the amount which the government takes. That, you *can* do. Easily, legally and cost-effectively.

Supposing you and your wife enjoy average age 70 and have an estate worth $10 million. When you die—remember, there's no "if" about it—the government will require approximately $5 million in estate taxes and your heirs will be left with $5 million.

But, if you were to purchase a last-to-die insurance policy, it would yield a guaranteed return, based on current assumptions, of 5–1. That means $1 million would produce $5 million and your heirs would be made whole. The government would take $5 million, but the insurance would produce $5 million which your heirs would receive income and estate tax free. Instead of receiving only $5 million—the remainder of your estate after the taxes are paid—they would receive $9.5 million.

Your $10 million estate would be reduced to $9 million after the transfer of $1 million to an irrevocable trust for the purchase of the insurance. The taxes on that $9 million would now be $4.5 million instead of $5 million leaving your children $4.5 million. But the insurance would produce $5 million following the death of the second spouse so your children would receive $5 million from the insurance plus the $4.5 million left from your estate for a total of $9.5 million. *That easily, the $5 million your children would have inherited has become almost $10 million.*

Furthermore, the cost of leaving your children virtually twice as well off isn't really $1 million. It's really only $50 thousand a year. Since you have $10 million, the chances are good and it is a fair assumption to make, that you would not ever spend the $1 million principal which you're transferring to the trust. You would, in all likelihood, use it only to produce interest income. Therefore, it is not really costing you $1 million but rather the $50 thousand which the $1 million would earn at 5% interest yearly.

If you need the additional $50 thousand interest income to support your lifestyle, you should not undertake this plan. But, if the $450 thousand which the remaining $9 million of your principal can be assumed to earn is sufficient to support you and your spouse in the manner to which you've become accustomed, there is no better use to which the $50 thousand could be put.

RECEIVE A 90% DISCOUNT ON YOUR ESTATE TAX COST

$495,800 Transferred to Irrevocable Trust Pays $4,948,000 Tax on your $10 Million Estate

**Transfer One Payment of
$495,800 or
$65,000 Yearly for 7 Years**

GAIN
$4,452,200

10 to 1 Return
$4,948,000

$3,000,000 ESTATE		AGE 60		AGE 70		AGE 80	
	Current	1 Pay	7 Pay	1 Pay	7 Pay	1 Pay	7 Pay
Estate Value	$3,000,000	$3,000,000	$3,000,000	$3,000,000	$3,000,000	$3,000,000	$3,000,000
Buy Insurance	$0	$1,100,000	$1,100,000	$1,100,000	$1,100,000	$1,100,000	$1,100,000
Cost of Ins.	$0	($142,187)	($24,094)	($228,200)	($39,101)	($323,961)	($57,702)
Gift Tax	$0	$0	$0	$0	$0	$0	$0
Discount	0%	87%	85%	79%	75%	71%	63%
Return	0	7.7 to 1	6.5 to 1	4.8 to 1	4 to 1	3.4 to 1	2.7 to 1
Estate Tax	($1,100,000)	($1,010,000)	($1,000,000)	($960,000)	($940,000)	($890,000)	($886,000)
Net to Family	$1,900,000	$2,957,813	$2,931,342	$2,911,800	$2,886,293	$2,886,039	$2,810,086

$10,000,000 ESTATE		AGE 60		AGE 70		AGE 80	
	Current	1 Pay	7 Pay	1 Pay	7 Pay	1 Pay	7 Pay
Estate Value	$10,000,000	$10,000,000	$10,000,000	$10,000,000	$10,000,000	$10,000,000	$10,000,000
Buy Insurance	$0	$5,000,000	$5,000,000	$5,000,000	$5,000,000	$5,000,000	$5,000,000
Cost of Ins.	$0	($643,786)	($109,089)	($1,035,078)	($177,352)	($1,470,815)	($261,976)
Gift Tax	$0	$0	$0	$0	$0	$0	$0
Discount	0%	87%	85%	79%	75%	71%	63%
Return	0	7.7 to 1	6.5 to 1	4.8 to 1	4 to 1	3.4 to 1	2.7 to 1
Estate Tax	($5,000,000)	($4,500,000)	($4,400,000)	($4,200,000)	($4,175,000)	($4,123,000)	($3,900,000)
Net to Family	$5,000,000	$9,856,214	$9,836,377	$9,764,922	$9,583,536	$9,406,185	$9,266,168

$50,000,000 ESTATE		AGE 60		AGE 70		AGE 80	
	Current	1 Pay	7 Pay	1 Pay	7 Pay	1 Pay	7 Pay
Estate Value	$50,000,000	$50,000,000	$50,000,000	$50,000,000	$50,000,000	$50,000,000	$50,000,000
Buy Insurance	$0	$27,500,000	$27,500,000	$27,500,000	$27,500,000	$27,500,000	$27,500,000
Cost of Ins.	$0	($3,537,628)	($599,446)	($5,690,143)	($974,958)	($8,087,279)	($1,440,482)
Gift Tax	$0	($1,768,814)	($2,098,061)	($2,845,072)	($3,412,353)	($4,043,640)	($5,041,687)
Discount	0%	87%	85%	79%	75%	71%	63%
Return	0	7.7 to 1	6.5 to 1	4.8 to 1	4 to 1	3.4 to 1	2.7 to 1
Estate Tax	($27,500,000)	($24,300,000)	($23,700,000)	($22,560,000)	($21,500,000)	($20,408,000)	($19,000,000)
Net to Family	$22,500,000	$47,893,558	$47,505,817	$46,404,785	$45,762,941	$44,969,108	$43,374,939

All figures are based on current assumptions. Charts are for illustrative purposes only.
©1994 WEALTH CREATION CENTERS℠ - Barry Kaye Associates

6

Double Your Gross Estate . . . Triple Your Net Estate

PUTTING YOUR MONEY TO WORK for you, having it earn more money, is what smart investing has always been about. You've probably given a lot of thought and consideration to the best means available for "growing" your principal. You've no doubt investigated the best stocks, the highest yield bonds, the most secure mutual funds. Yet, you've probably come to accept the fact that there are no guarantees. The complex economies of today's world are a challenge to even the most informed, adept investors and advisors.

If you were told that there was one investment opportunity that was *guaranteed*, based on current assumptions, to double your gross estate and triple your net estate, you might be skeptical, but you'd undoubtedly want to know more. Well, there is. *There is one investment that can double your gross and triple your net worth, and that is simple, legal and offers this fantastic return from the first day that you buy it!* That investment is life insurance and its return is guaranteed because your death is guaranteed to happen.

Let's assume that you and your spouse are 60 years old and have spent your lifetime amassing an estate worth $10 million. If you were to transfer $1 million to an irrevocable trust and that trust were to purchase a life insurance policy at a 10 to 1 return, at your death the insurance policy would pay your heirs $10 million. *Plus, they would still receive the remaining $9 million from your estate. That simply, you have doubled your gross estate!*

It would take you years, probably more years than you realistically have left, if it was possible at all, to effect that same 100% return on your investment. But, the life insurance policy will pay its return even if you die tomorrow.

Now consider this. If you did not take advantage of the incredible leverage of life insurance, your original $10 million estate would be subject to estate taxes of 50%, or $5 million. This would leave your heirs only $5 million net.

But by transferring the $1 million to the irrevocable trust and purchasing the $10 million of insurance, your heirs receive triple the net amount!

Remember, without the insurance, your heirs will receive $5 million after estate taxes are paid on your $10 million estate. With the insurance, they will receive $4.5 million from your original estate—you had $9 million left after transferring the $1 million to the trust and it was taxed at 50% leaving $4.5 million for your heirs—plus the $10 million in life insurance proceeds which they receive tax free. They receive a total of $14.5 million, *virtually triple the net amount they would have received otherwise!*

DOUBLE YOUR GROSS ESTATE
TRIPLE YOUR NET ESTATE

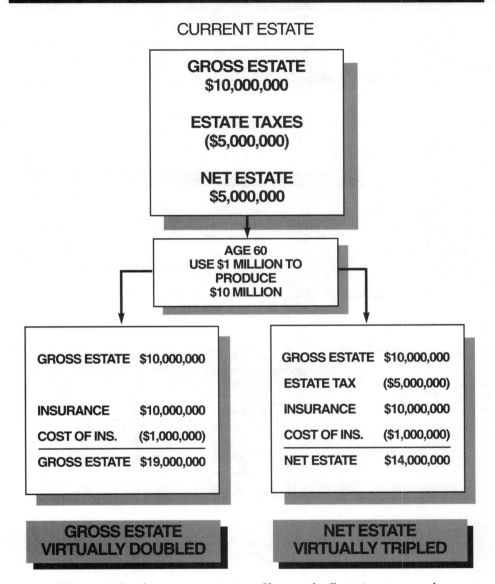

CURRENT ESTATE

GROSS ESTATE
$10,000,000

ESTATE TAXES
($5,000,000)

NET ESTATE
$5,000,000

AGE 60
USE $1 MILLION TO
PRODUCE
$10 MILLION

GROSS ESTATE	$10,000,000
INSURANCE	$10,000,000
COST OF INS.	($1,000,000)
GROSS ESTATE	$19,000,000

GROSS ESTATE	$10,000,000
ESTATE TAX	($5,000,000)
INSURANCE	$10,000,000
COST OF INS.	($1,000,000)
NET ESTATE	$14,000,000

GROSS ESTATE
VIRTUALLY DOUBLED

NET ESTATE
VIRTUALLY TRIPLED

All figures are based on current assumptions. Charts are for illustrative purposes only.
This illustration used a last-to-die insurance policy for a male and female both age 60.
©1994 WEALTH CREATION CENTERS℠ - Barry Kaye Associates

$3,000,000 ESTATE

	Current	AGE 60 1 Pay	AGE 70 1 Pay	AGE 80 1 Pay
Gross Estate	$3,000,000	$3,000,000	$3,000,000	$3,000,000
Buy Insurance	$0	$3,000,000	$3,000,000	$3,000,000
Cost of Insurance	$0	($386,555)	($621,295)	($882,684)
Gift Tax	$0	$0	$0	$0
Gross Estate	$3,000,000	$5,613,445	$5,378,705	$5,117,316
Estate Tax	($1,100,000)	($893,126)	($773,565)	($645,485)
Net Estate	$1,900,000	$4,720,319	$4,605,140	$4,471,831

$10,000,000 ESTATE

	Current	AGE 60 1 Pay	AGE 70 1 Pay	AGE 80 1 Pay
Gross Estate	$10,000,000	$10,000,000	$10,000,000	$10,000,000
Buy Insurance	$0	$10,000,000	$10,000,000	$10,000,000
Cost of Insurance	$0	($1,286,862)	($2,069,537)	($2,941,140)
Gift Tax	$0	$0	($1,034,769)	($1,470,570)
Gross Estate	$10,000,000	$18,713,138	$16,895,694	$15,588,290
Estate Tax	($5,000,000)	($4,240,226)	($3,240,632)	($2,521,560)
Net Estate	$5,000,000	$14,472,912	$13,655,062	$13,066,730

$50,000,000 ESTATE

	Current	AGE 60 1 Pay	AGE 70 1 Pay	AGE 80 1 Pay
Gross Estate	$50,000,000	$50,000,000	$50,000,000	$50,000,000
Buy Insurance	$0	$50,000,000	$50,000,000	$50,000,000
Cost of Insurance	$0	($6,431,474)	($10,345,213)	($14,703,744)
Gift Tax	$0	($3,215,737)	($5,172,607)	($7,351,872)
Gross Estate	$50,000,000	$90,352,789	$84,482,180	$77,944,384
Estate Tax	($27,500,000)	($22,194,034)	($18,965,199)	($15,369,411)
Net Estate	$22,500,000	$68,158,755	$65,516,981	$62,574,973

All figures are based on current assumptions. Charts are for illustrative purposes only.
©1994 WEALTH CREATION CENTERS℠ - Barry Kaye Associates

7

Generation Skipping Trust— Build a 100-Year Tax Free Estate

You love your children and you want to provide the greatest possible level of financial security for them. That's why you're considering establishing an irrevocable trust on their behalf and gifting it with enough money to purchase a life insurance policy that will fully replace any estate taxes that threaten their inheritance.

But what about your grandchildren, and their children? Wouldn't it be great if you could gift your assets to them, through the generations, without the decimation of estate taxes, creating a legacy of security that could survive intact for 100 years? Well, you can! Simply by taking advantage of the current generation skipping transfer tax exemption, you can ensure that your estate will pass to your children, their children and their children's children (in legal terms: this generation and any living generations plus 21 years) without being reduced even $1 by estate taxes. In effect, *you can create a $1 million, $10 million, $50 million or even greater trust that will not be subject to any estate taxes over approximately the next 100 years!*

To accomplish this goal, you would transfer $1.2 million to a generation skipping trust. Assuming that you and your spouse have not previously utilized your combined $1.2 million exemptions, there will be no gift tax. Furthermore, if you skip a generation and leave the money directly for the benefit of your grandchildren, you and your spouse are both allowed to gift $1 million each with no generation skipping transfer tax. If you have already utilized some of your initial exemption, you would then pay the appropriate gift taxes or even generation skipping tax to accommodate this approach.

If you and your spouse are age 60 when you transfer the $1.2 million to the generation skipping trust, it will fully fund a life insurance policy paying proceeds of $12 million to the trust for your family at your deaths. If you are age 70, the $1.2 million gift will fund $6 million. At age 80 it will fund $3.6 million. If you choose to utilize a generation skipping trust, you and your wife are allowed to transfer $1 million each without any generation skipping transfer tax for a total transfer of $2 million and, at age 60, it will produce a return of $20 million for your grandchildren. At age 70, the return is $10 million and at age 80 it is $6 million.

When you utilize a generation skipping trust, it means the principal remains in the trust throughout the trust's duration. Since the principal is not removed from the trust, it is not subject to any estate taxes. However, each generation of heirs may receive the income which the principal produces. In this manner *you can create income producing, estate tax free assets of $12 million—or the appropriate amount as indicated above—for your children with no additional estate taxes until after the death of the third generation*—approximately one hundred years down the road under current law.

If you really wish to optimize this concept, you and your spouse can also take advantage of the combined $2 million generation skipping transfer exemption to create huge wealth for your grandchildren and their children and the rest of your progeny for years to come.

Using this approach, you could use your combined $1.2 million gift or transfer tax exemption, or any part thereof, to insure your own lives on behalf of your children. As stated above, this $1.2 million would produce, depending on your age, a 3–10 times return—$3.6 million to $12 million—estate tax free for 100 years.

You and your spouse could then use the combined balance of your $2 million generation skipping transfer exemption to insure the lives of your children on behalf of your grandchildren. Since your children are younger, the return on their policy would be closer to 40–50 times the policy's cost producing an astonishing additional $32 million–$40 million into the generation skipping trust on an estate tax free basis for the benefit of your grandchildren and their children! This truly builds a family dynasty. Naturally, the amount of insurance you can purchase may be limited to the extent that the various insurance companies allow you and your children to purchase large amounts of coverage based upon your assets or projected assets.

Just imagine. If your children used some of the income proceeds from the $12 million which the trust held to purchase insurance on their children or grandchildren, and set up generation skipping trusts of their own, and their children did the same and their children did the same, *the legacy you create could continue in perpetuity blessing your family with the gift of financial security virtually forever.*

Of course, you are not limited to amounts of $1.2 million or $2 million (in regard to establishing a generation skipping trust). These are simply the amounts you can gift without having to pay estate transfer, gift or generation skipping taxes. And even if you have already used all or some portion of your exemption amounts, *it is entirely possible that the benefits to be reaped by utilizing larger amounts of transferred funds will significantly override the cost of paying the gift tax.* You can also give smaller amounts and your family will still enjoy a great future security. Your individual situation would have to be analyzed to determine the best course of action.

GENERATION SKIPPING TRANSFER TAX

Basic use of the GSTT

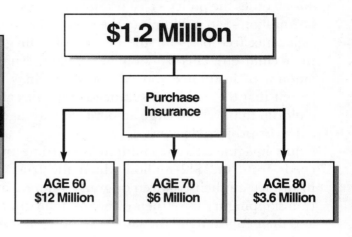

Use $1.2 million generation skipping trust to purchase a last-to-die life **INSURANCE POLICY ON YOURSELF** for the benefit of your grandchildren

$1.2 Million

Purchase Insurance

AGE 60	AGE 70	AGE 80
$12 Million	$6 Million	$3.6 Million

Maximum use of the GSTT

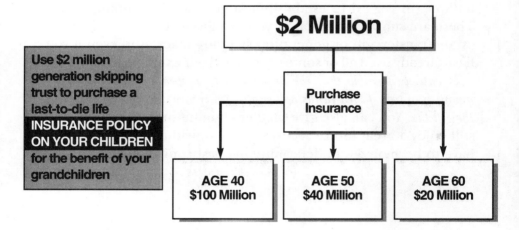

Use $2 million generation skipping trust to purchase a last-to-die life **INSURANCE POLICY ON YOUR CHILDREN** for the benefit of your grandchildren

$2 Million

Purchase Insurance

AGE 40	AGE 50	AGE 60
$100 Million	$40 Million	$20 Million

All figures are based on current assumptions. Charts are for illustrative purposes only.

©1994 WEALTH CREATION CENTERS℠ - Barry Kaye Associates

8

Increase Charitable Contributions up to 10 Times at no Additional Cost

IF YOU HAVE SLATED some portion of your estate to ultimately be gifted to charity and were told that, at no additional cost to you, that gift could be increased 3, 5, even 10 times, you'd be ecstatic wouldn't you? Of course, you would. Who wouldn't want to do 10 times as much good with the same principal amount? Who wouldn't enjoy the thought of leaving behind a tenfold legacy of charitable works?

What if you were further told that you could accomplish this philanthropic miracle without having to risk any of your own financial security? That you could retain the availability of the donated funds throughout your lifetime or could receive the income tax benefit of having made the contribution right away? Would you be interested? You bet you would!

Well, it is all possible, even easy. Here's how.

Let's assume that you are 70 years old and have set aside $5 million to be given to the charity of your choice upon your death. Let's further assume that you don't need the approximately $250 thousand of interest income which this $5 million produces annually to sustain your everyday lifestyle.

By purchasing a life insurance policy which named the charity as beneficiary, you could ultimately gift the charity $25 million for a $5 million one-time payment. That's because, at age 70, the policy could be expected to yield a 5–1 return. If you were 60, your $5 million donation could become $50 million and if you were 80, it would produce a 3–1 return of $15 million.

Furthermore, because you have removed the principal from your estate and assigned it to a charity or charitable foundation, you will be able to deduct the full policy cost from your income tax. *That's a $5 million income tax deduction from which you can benefit immediately in addition to a strongly optimized charitable contribution to be made upon your death.* And, since the $5 million has been gifted to charity, it is not subject to estate taxes, either.

But maybe you would prefer not to transfer the $5 million out of your possession at this time. Though you don't need the income it produces to preserve your day-to-day standard of living, maybe you're concerned about the future. In an emergency, the $250 thousand per year income which the $5 million principal can be assumed to produce might be needed.

In that case, you could hold the policy within your estate as an excellent asset with substantial cash values. This will provide you with emergency security while you live; the policy will ultimately be transferred to your charity at your death. In this way, *you get the best of both worlds: a significantly optimized charitable donation and retention of the asset's equity during your lifetime for any unforeseen emergency.*

GIVE MORE TO CHARITY

AGE 60 - $1 GIVES $10

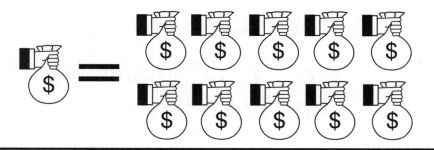

AGE 70 - $1 GIVES $5

AGE 80 - $1 GIVES $3

All figures are based on current assumptions. Charts are for illustrative purposes only.

©1994 WEALTH CREATION CENTERS℠ - Barry Kaye Associates

9

=====

Turn "Junk" Money
Into Huge Money

THROUGHOUT THIS BOOK, you are told that, wonderful as the opportunities presented here are, you should not participate in them if the cost of doing so would in any way negatively impact your current lifestyle. As much as you may want to discount your estate tax costs and provide financial security for your children and grandchildren, as much as you may desire to optimize your charitable donations, as much as you would like to recover previous investment losses or hedge against the certainty of a grievous loss to come, *providing for your own immediate needs and desires must come first.*

But there does come a point in many estate situations, where you have amassed enough principal that the interest it earns is more than enough to provide for the continuation of your present lifestyle. A time when your "pile" of money is big enough that the dollars on the bottom are unnecessary to sustain your way of life. These bills are often referred to as discretionary, surplus, or excess money—what is referred to here as "junk" money. Some people don't even realize they have junk money; it may be sitting in miscellaneous stocks, old investments which have lost their glitter, savings accounts which have accumulated for years.

If you have such discretionary funds in your estate, the chances are that you are intending them for the future benefit of your heirs. But, *as long as those funds remain in your estate, they will be subject to estate taxes at your death and, as such, are worth considerably less to your heirs.* Depending on the size of your estate, they will be subject to taxes ranging from 37% to 60% which means your heirs will actually receive only 63% to 40% of their current financial value. This is truly junk money because you won't spend the principal, you don't need the income it produces to support your lifestyle, the government takes 55% of it upon your death and your family receives only 45%. That's about as junky as you can get!

But that same "junk" money can be used to protect the full value of your estate so you can pass it on intact to your children. Not only can it be utilized to recoup its own principal value, but it can also protect the entire amount of your principal from the ravages of estate taxation. All at virtually no cost to you, since you do not have need of the funds anyway.

If you are worth $20 million, your estate will be taxed 55% of its total worth upon your death; estate taxes will take $11 million from your heirs. If you and your spouse are an average 60 years old, a one-pay, last-to-die insurance policy would cost approximately $1.1 million, based on current assumptions. Transferred to an irrevocable trust, the money spent to purchase the policy would produce its $11 million return income and estate tax free to your heirs, fully replacing the entire estate taxes. In addition, since together you and your spouse have a $1.2 million estate and gift tax exemption, you would pay no gift tax on the transferred $1.1 million. If you used the entire $1.2 million to purchase an insurance policy, you could recover not only the estate taxes but the cost of the policy as well!

Having an estate of $20 million, it is very likely that you do not need the approximate $55 thousand of income which the "bottom" $1.1 million is producing annually. If that is so, you could easily reallocate the "junk" money to the purpose of funding lasting financial security for your heirs. Not only would you increase the value of the discretionary funds, but you would protect the full value of your entire estate. And all this is accomplished using money you did not need anyway.

Why would you want to leave your children $9 million—the eventual value of your $20 million estate less the $11 million in estate taxes which will be levied upon your death—when you could leave them the full $20 million? Where else could you possibly invest that $55 thousand and receive a return of $11 million the first year, the first week if need be? Nowhere. Nowhere.

Remember, if you do not use this plan to create the $12 million, your "junk" money will be worth, at your death after taxes, only $540 thousand. *$540 thousand or $12 million—it shouldn't be a difficult choice to make!*

$11 MILLION OFF THE TOP
OR
$1.1 MILLION OFF THE BOTTOM

$20 Million Estate

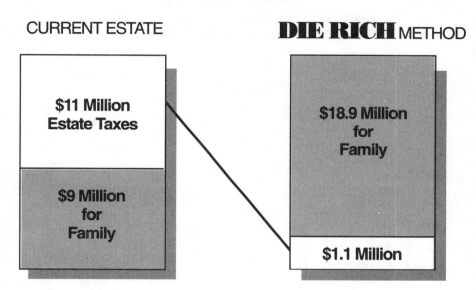

CURRENT ESTATE

DIE RICH METHOD

$11 Million Estate Taxes

$9 Million for Family

$18.9 Million for Family

$1.1 Million

The $1.1 million of junk money "off the bottom" is used to purchase a last-to-die life insurance policy that will produce $11 million to pay the estate taxes.

Junk Money is excess-surplus-discretionary money you no longer wish to risk, thus you no longer need the principal or the income it produces in excess of what your lifestyle requires.

Uncle Sam receives 55% and your family gets 45%.

That's about as junky as it gets!

THE CHOICE IS YOURS!

CONVERT YOUR JUNK MONEY

Junk Money is excess-surplus-discretionary money you no longer wish to risk, thus you no longer need the principal or the income it produces in excess of what your lifestyle requires.

Uncle Sam gets 55% and your family gets 45%.
That's about as junky as it gets!

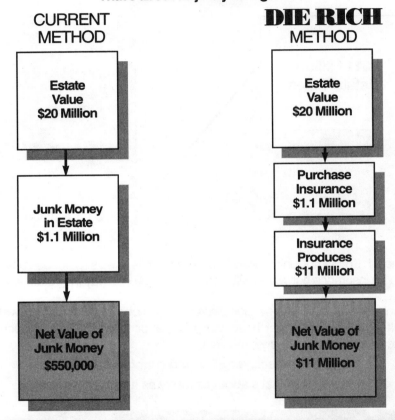

CURRENT METHOD

Estate
Value
$20 Million

Junk Money
in Estate
$1.1 Million

Net Value of
Junk Money
$550,000

DIE RICH METHOD

Estate
Value
$20 Million

Purchase
Insurance
$1.1 Million

Insurance
Produces
$11 Million

Net Value of
Junk Money
$11 Million

$550,000 OR $11 MILLION?

All figures are based on current assumptions. Charts are for illustrative purposes only.
This illustration used a last-to-die insurance policy for a male and female both age 60.
©1994 WEALTH CREATION CENTERS℠ - Barry Kaye Associates

$3,000,000 ESTATE

	Current	AGE 60 1 Pay	AGE 70 1 Pay	AGE 80 1 Pay
Estate Size	$3,000,000	$3,000,000	$3,000,000	$3,000,000
Estate Tax	$0	($1,100,000)	($1,100,000)	($1,100,000)
Buy Insurance	$0	$1,100,000	$1,100,000	$1,100,000
Cost of Insurance	$0	($142,187)	($228,200)	($323,961)
Gift Tax	$0	$0	$0	$0
Junk Money Value	$0	$71,094	$114,100	$161,981
Converted Value	$0	$1,100,000	$1,100,000	$1,100,000

$10,000,000 ESTATE

	Current	AGE 60 1 Pay	AGE 70 1 Pay	AGE 80 1 Pay
Estate Size	$10,000,000	$10,000,000	$10,000,000	$10,000,000
Estate Tax	$0	($5,000,000)	($5,000,000)	($5,000,000)
Buy Insurance	$0	$5,000,000	$5,000,000	$5,000,000
Cost of Insurance	$0	($643,786)	($1,035,078)	($1,470,815)
Gift Tax	$0	$0	$0	$0
Junk Money Value	$0	$321,893	$517,539	$735,408
Converted Value	$0	$5,000,000	$5,000,000	$5,000,000

$50,000,000 ESTATE

	Current	AGE 60 1 Pay	AGE 70 1 Pay	AGE 80 1 Pay
Estate Size	$50,000,000	$50,000,000	$50,000,000	$50,000,000
Estate Tax	$0	($27,500,000)	($27,500,000)	($27,500,000)
Buy Insurance	$0	$27,500,000	$27,500,000	$27,500,000
Cost of Insurance	$0	($3,537,628)	($5,690,143)	($8,087,279)
Gift Tax	$0	($1,768,814)	($2,845,072)	($4,043,640)
Junk Money Value	$0	$2,653,221	$4,267,608	$6,065,460
Converted Value	$0	$27,500,000	$27,500,000	$27,500,000

All figures are based on current assumptions. Charts are for illustrative purposes only.
©1994 WEALTH CREATION CENTERS℠ - Barry Kaye Associates

10

When Will the Stock Market Crash 2000 Points?

IF YOU KNEW THE DAY the stock market would crash 2000 points from 3,600 to 1,600, what would you do? There is only one answer: Sell, and sell short if you are aggressive, to hedge the market.

The trick, of course, is to know when the market will crash. But it's really not a trick at all. **The day the market crashes is the day you die.** Guaranteed. Estate taxes will decimate your portfolio as surely as a 2000 point stock market plunge. They will reduce the value of your assets a guaranteed minimum of 37% assuming your total estate is worth $3 million or more. They could reduce its value by as much as 55%.

If you agree that you would hedge a potentially devastating loss you knew was coming, then why wouldn't you hedge the guaranteed loss of your stocks, bonds, real estate and other assets which will certainly occur at the moment of your death?

Your $60/each shares of AT&T are worth only $27 if you are holding them for your heirs and do not need the principal to support your own lifestyle. The stock *must double* between now and the day you die, which realistically could be tomorrow, in order for it to simply retain its current market value for your beneficiaries. By this same model, your $80/each shares of Paramount may be worth only $36 per share to your heirs! That's a loss of $44 per share. If you knew Paramount would drop $44 per share in a day, you'd frantically cry "Sell!" as loudly as you could. Well, that day *will* come. It's inescapable. But *there is a hedge against this devastating loss.*

Let's say you and your wife are average age 70 years old, you own stocks currently valued at $4 million and you do not need the principal asset of those stocks to maintain your current lifestyle. At your death, those stocks will only be worth $1.8 million to your heirs; they will lose $2.2 million to estate taxation. But, if you were to sell $440 thousand worth of stock and transfer the proceeds to an irrevocable trust, the trust could purchase a life insurance policy which, upon your death, would pay five times the purchase price, $2.2 million, to your heirs thereby replacing the $2.2 million which the government will take in estate taxes. Your investments would be fully hedged and protected and your heirs would inherit their full value. Since you did not need the $4 million to support your lifestyle, the sale of $440 thousand worth of stock will not negatively impact you in any way yet it will have a tremendously positive affect on the success of your portfolio and on the financial security of your heirs. You have created your own guaranteed hedge fund.

Upon your deaths, as indicated above, the $60 AT&T stock would be worth only $27. You could have sold the $60 stock and purchased, based on age 60 last-to-die, $600 worth of insurance. Your $60 stock would have go to $1,200 per share in order to be worth the $600 after tax that you accomplish by purchasing the insurance. Do you really think your $60 AT&T is going to $1,200? If you don't, why would you hold $60 AT&T that is only going to be worth $27 when you can immediately make it worth effectively $1,200 a share at your death? Even at age 70, a $300 last-to-die policy can be purchased rather than retaining the AT&T stock which will ultimately be worth only $27. In this instance, the stock would have to go to $600 to be equal to the insurance value at your death. And finally, if you and your wife are 80, you could purchase $180 insurance which means your stock would have to go to $360 per share to net for your heirs, upon your deaths, the same return. *If you don't really believe that the $60 AT&T is going to grow to $1,200* *per share, $600 per share or $360 per share, why would you hold on to it when there is such a simple way of making it worth so much more!*

Using the same method, you can also recover any loss you may have already experienced.

Suppose you had purchased $6 million of real estate with money not necessary to keep up your standard of living and that real estate was now worth only $5 million. Through the vagaries of the market, you've lost $1 million. Or, more concisely, your heirs have lost $1 million; since you didn't need the $6 million anyway, it is safe to assume that you were protecting it for your heirs' ultimate inheritance.

If you and your wife are 60 years old, you could transfer $100 thousand to an irrevocable trust and purchase a life insurance policy which, at a 10 to 1 return, would, upon your death, replace the $1 million of devalued real estate you worked so hard to amass. Your heirs would inherit the full $6 million which you originally intended them to have!

You can even use this method to recover the cost of the insurance itself. By selling slightly more stock than you need to cover the estate tax cost or investment loss, you can effectively discount the cost of the insurance by ⅓, ⅕ or ⅒ of the purchase price depending on your age. For example, if you're 60 years old and you need to recover a $2 million loss, the insurance policy would cost approximately $200 thousand. If you were to sell enough stock to cover this $200 thousand cost plus an additional $20 thousand, you would recover the $200 thousand policy cost also. In this manner, $200 thousand effectively recovers the full $2 million investment loss and the $20 thousand buys an extra $200 thousand which covers the insurance cost.

Though you or your financial advisors may not have considered the situation from this vantage point before, it is a completely accurate, legal and simple perspective. So, why wouldn't you want to hedge the certain, tragic—and completely avoidable—loss of up to 55% of your stock, bond and real estate assets when, for ⅒ or even 1/100 of the potential loss, you could insure your investments and protect their full, current value?

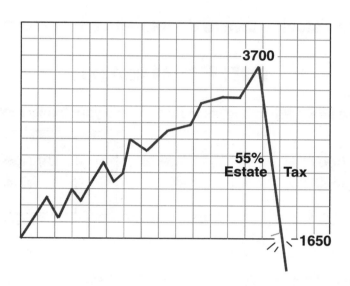

THE DAY YOU DIE!

All figures are based on current assumptions. Charts are for illustrative purposes only.

©1994 WEALTH CREATION CENTERS℠ - Barry Kaye Associates

THE STOCK MARKET CRASH

AT&T now worth $60 a share
is worth $27 a share—the day you die

Your stocks have to double—just to stay even!

DIE RICH METHOD

Use the same $60 to buy life insurance and your family receives:

At Age 60 $600	At Age 70 $300	At Age 80 $180

To equal the Die Rich Method, AT&T would have to reach:

At Age 60 $1,200 a share	At Age 70 $600 a share	At Age 80 $360 a share

IF YOU THINK $60 AT&T IS GOING TO REACH
$360 - $1,200 PER SHARE – DON'T BUY INSURANCE!

All figures are based on current assumptions. Charts are for illustrative purposes only.

11

Sell All Depreciated Assets for the Same Value They Had 3 Years Ago

No ONE IS IMMUNE to recessionary times. Depreciation of assets strikes everyone. But *there is a way to fully recover lost asset value, to "turn back the clock" and still receive for your assets what they were worth before the recession took its toll.*

Consider the case of a man who bought some undeveloped real estate twenty years ago. Three years ago, he was offered $80 million for the parcel but he turned it down anticipating that its value would continue to increase to $100 million. He looked forward eagerly to the fullest appreciation of his investment. Then, the recession hit and now his land is only worth $50 million.

This man bemoans the loss of the additional $30 million he could have made; he is angry and sad to have lost $30 million while he was waiting for it to reach $100 million.

But the truth is, even if he had sold the real estate when he was offered $80 million, if it was his intention that the principal be held for his children's ultimate benefit, it would never have been worth more than $27 million. Capital gains tax on the profit he had earned would have taken $20 million. Estate taxes on the remaining $60 million would claim an additional $33 million. The real value of the asset to his children would be the remaining $27 million!

There is a way for the man to effectively achieve not only the $80 million he was once offered, but the full $100 million he thought the land would ultimately be worth . . . *a way to increase the value of his asset 3 or 4 times over today's depreciated assessment.*

The man is 78 years old, his wife is 68. Together they enjoy an average age of 72 which will allow them approximately a 5–1 return on a one-pay, last-to-die insurance policy, based on current assumptions.

If the man were to sell the property today, he would receive $50 million. He would pay $15 million capital gains tax on the sale amount leaving him approximately $35 million. If he transfers $23 million to an irrevocable trust and the trust purchases a life insurance policy at a 5–1 return, it will produce $100 million. That $100 million will come to his heirs income and estate tax free, accomplishing for him what he originally set out to do. His heirs will inherit not only the $80 million which was the best offer he ever received for the land, but the full $100 million which he thought it would ultimately be worth—and it will come to them tax free. The remaining $12 million from the $35 million after tax sale proceeds, would pay the gift tax on the $23 million transfer in full thus allowing the entire $100 million to come in estate tax free. They pay only $12 million gift tax on the $23 million transfer rather than $55 million on the $100 million at their deaths.

The man's highest and best hopes had been for his property to reach $100 million in value. Yet, even if it had, his children would only have received $30 million after capital gains and estate taxes. Now, they will receive the full $100 million tax free!

It's never to late. Utilizing the leverage of life insurance and the tax advantages contained therein can make up many missed opportunities.

SELL FOR LESS
RECEIVE 3 1/2 TIMES MORE

	CURRENT METHOD	DIE RICH METHOD
Sell Property	$80,000,000	$50,000,000
Capital Gains Tax	($20,000,000)	($15,000,000)
Net Assets	$60,000,000	$35,000,000
Buy $100 Million of Insurance	$0	($22,000,000)
Gift Tax	$0	($13,000,000)
Estate Tax	($33,000,000)	$0
Insurance Pays	$0	$100,000,000
Net to Family	$27,000,000	$100,000,000

IT'S NEVER TOO LATE TO SELL!

All figures are based on current assumptions. Charts are for illustrative purposes only.
This illustration used a last-to-die insurance policy for a male and female both age 70.
©1994 WEALTH CREATION CENTERS℠ - Barry Kaye Associates

12

Recover All Liquidity

IT IS A COMMON MISCONCEPTION that only illiquid estates need life insurance. Many people assume that if they are liquid their financial holdings will be sufficient to pay off the estate taxes which will be due nine months after their death and therefore they don't need the coverage insurance provides. It is only the illiquid, they assume, who are in jeopardy of needing a loan to pay off the estate taxes or who might have to sell property at forced liquidation prices, who need insurance. "Why should I," the liquid muse, "deplete my liquid assets buying protection for those same assets?" They think, "It just doesn't make any sense to spend money to save money."

This thinking could not be further from the truth.

In fact, both liquid and illiquid estates are at risk from the costs of estate taxation. While it is true that illiquid estates face greater ravages due to the costs of financing the estate tax debt or liquidating assets to raise the needed capital, the liquid suffer the same percentage "loss" of their gross estates to estate taxation.

Consider this:

One man has $19 million of real estate, is illiquid and therefore purchases a life insurance policy as an investment to protect his estate. As he and his wife are average age 60, $1 million purchases a $10 million policy, based on current assumptions. After the death of the man and his wife, the government assesses $10 million of taxes on his $19 million worth of real estate. Instead of having to take a loan against the property or sell it for a fraction of its value in order to pay the taxes, his heirs receive $10 million from the insurance policy and use it to pay the taxes at an effective 90% discount. *They inherit, intact, the full $19 million of real estate and pay the taxes for only the $1 million cost of the policy.*

Another man has the same $19 million in *liquid assets*: CD's, T-Bills, Municipal Bonds, etc. Thinking he has the liquidity to pay the taxes, he decides against the purchase of life insurance. He doesn't see a reason to spend the needed $1 million to protect his estate when it is already protected by his liquid assets.

Upon the death of the second man and his wife, the government assesses $10 million in estate taxes. Though his heirs have the "cash" to pay the taxes, they are left with only $9 million. The man's "saved" $1 million cost his family $9 million.

The end result is that the illiquid man left his family the full $19 million of his estate while the liquid man left his family only $9 million. And what is particularly ridiculous is that the liquid man could have very easily come up with the $1 million in one-pay insurance premium. Furthermore, his true expense would really only have been the $50 thousand a year income which the $1 million could be assumed to earn in interest. The idea isn't to be liquid in order to meet the tax bill, but to discount the estate tax cost.

Save $50 thousand a year in order to eventually lose $10 million. Somehow, it doesn't seem to make much sense.

LIQUIDITY CAN BE DANGEROUS

LIQUID ASSET

vs.

ILLIQUID ASSET

	LIQUID ASSET	ILLIQUID ASSET
Estate Value	$20,000,000	$20,000,000
Insurance Cost	$0	($1,100,000)
Insurance Pays	$0	$11,000,000
Estate Taxes	($11,000,000)	($11,000,000)
Net to Family	$9,000,000	$18,900,000)

THE PRICE OF LIQUIDITY IS $9.9 MILLION

All figures are based on current assumptions. Charts are for illustrative purposes only.
This illustration used a last-to-die insurance policy for a male and female both age 60.
©1994 WEALTH CREATION CENTERS℠ - Barry Kaye Associates

13

Leverage Your IRA or Pension
Ten to Twenty Times

Dɪᴅ ʏᴏᴜ ᴋɴᴏᴡ that if you have amassed a $1 million pension or
IRA, it may really be worth only $270 thousand?

If it is your intention to eventually claim the benefit of your
pension and use it to support your lifestyle, you are certainly
entitled to do so. You earned that money and its first purpose must
be to fulfill your needs and desires. But if these funds are excess
funds that you don't need for income and you have been thinking
of them as a legacy to your heirs, you better think again.

When you die, if you are worth over $3 million, thus exposing
you to a 55% estate tax bracket, your $1 million IRA or pension
will be subject to income taxes of approximately $400 thousand.
That will leave $600 thousand upon which your heirs will pay $330
thousand in estate taxes. They'll inherit only $270 thousand as the
full total dollar representation of all your hard work. *Less than one
third of your intended gift will ever reach your children's hands!*

But there is a better way. A way to not only ensure that your
children receive the full $1 million but to ultimately increase that
$1 million to approximately $5 million which your heirs will receive income and estate tax free. Here's how:

Terminate the pension plan or IRA now and take the $1 million.
You'll have to pay income taxes of $400 thousand, but, as long as

your children are going to eventually receive $5 million anyway, it's not the end of the world. And it's certainly better than paying $730 thousand in combined income and estate taxes while your heirs only receive $270 thousand.

Place the remaining $600 thousand into an irrevocable trust and use it to fund the purchase of a one-pay, last-to-die life insurance policy. Depending on your age, health, and marital status, that policy will pay your heirs a greatly optimized return of $5 million! *That's almost 20 times the $270 thousand they would have otherwise received.*

Even if you retained your IRA and it increased in value to an impossible $20 million, your children would still not get the same return!

An IRA worth $20 million would be subject to excise tax of 15%, or $3 million, leaving $17 million. The $20 million would then be subject to income taxes of approximately 40%, $8 million. In this way, the $20 million would be decreased to only $9 million. After being subjected to a 50% estate tax of $4.5 million, that $9 million would net your heirs only $4.5 million.

Remember, even if some miracle were to occur that would allow a $1 million IRA to increase to $20 million, it would have to do so within your remaining life expectancy for your children to derive any benefit. But the *guaranteed miracle of life insurance* will pay them the same return whether you die 25 years from now, a month from now, or tomorrow.

It's your choice—$270 thousand or $5 million for your heirs from the same $1 million IRA or pension fund.

INCREASE YOUR IRA OR PENSION 10 - 20 TIMES

	CURRENT METHOD	DIE RICH METHOD	INVESTMENT METHOD
IRA / Pension	$1,000,000	$1,000,000	$1,000,000
Asset Increase	$0	$0	$19,000,000
Excise Tax	$0	$0	($3,000,000)
Income Tax	($400,000)	($400,000)	($8,000,000)
Net Assets	$600,000	$600,000	$9,000,000
Purchase Insurance $5 Million Death Benefit	$0	($600,000)	$0
Estate Tax	($330,000)	$0	($5,000,000)
Insurance Pays	$0	$5,000,000	$0
Net To Family	$270,000	$5,000,000	$4,000,000

$270,000 OR $5 MILLION . . . WHICH DO YOU WANT FOR YOUR FAMILY?

All figures are based on current assumptions. Charts are for illustrative purposes only.
This illustration used a last-to-die insurance policy for a male and female both age 65.
©1994 WEALTH CREATION CENTERS℠ - Barry Kaye Associates

14

Increase Yields Up to 20%

MUNICIPAL BONDS HAVE NO RESPECT for age. The pay the same 5% interest whether you are 30, 50 or 80. The same is true of CD's and T-bills which also currently produce only about 5%—less, after taxes. There is no consideration for age in any of these vehicles. It does not matter if you will collect the interest for 50 years or 15.

But it should matter to you as you are making your financial plans. *If you are older and your concern is not for your principal but for the interest income it produces, why would you settle for 5% when you could be earning 3, even 4 times more?*

Using an immediate annuity, your yield actually increases the older or more ill you are, based on current taxes and life expectancy. It may seem a somewhat distasteful subject, but, with so much at stake, it is well worth discussing. Since an immediate annuity pays its promised return for the rest of your life, the shorter that timespan is calculated to be, the higher the return that is offered. And the increased sums which are produced by the higher payments can, in turn, be utilized in a myriad number of ways to create and preserve wealth, to increase charitable donations many times, to pay for increased medical expenses, etc. *They can even be used to recover the full principal amount for the benefit of your heirs. In this way, you would have greater income for the rest of your life and your heirs would not lose a dime of their intended inheritance!*

When you purchase an immediate annuity, the principal

amount with which the purchase is made vanishes from your holdings. It is used in full to support the higher principal and interest returns which the annuity provides. But, for the rest of your life, that principal will be used to produce income of 15%–20%!

If you have $5 million in municipal bonds producing 5% per year, your asset is earning only $250 thousand annually. Upon your death, estate taxes on the $5 million will be about $2.7 million leaving only $2.3 million for your children to inherit.

At age 80, an immediate annuity purchased with the same $5 million could yield as much as $750 thousand per year—a 15% return which triples your interest income. This increased income can then be used to more than recover the $2.3 million which your children would have inherited from your original $5 million in bonds.

At age 80, $2.3 million in insurance would cost approximately $115 thousand per year. This would leave $635 thousand, still more than the twice the income your municipal bonds had been earning. *Your income would have increased dramatically and your children would still receive the full inheritance you had intended for them.*

But you need not leave it at that. If the $250 thousand which the bonds were producing was sufficient to support your lifestyle, you could take the entire difference, or any portion thereof, and use it to purchase insurance on behalf of your heirs. The immediate annuity is producing $500 thousand per year more than the bonds were. That $500 thousand, if used to purchased insurance on you for the benefit of your children, could ultimately produce $10 million, based on current assumptions. *Your children would not only receive the full inheritance they would have before . . . they will not only recover the estate tax costs to inherit the entire value of your estate . . . they will receive virtually double your estate's current value income and estate tax free!*

There will be numerous opportunities for you to optimize the increased income. You could hold some of the income in your estate against emergency need or to enhance your lifestyle. You could, as described above, use the difference to create wealth for your children. You could use the difference to create a legacy of financial security for your grandchildren. *Or you could do all three.*

Your immediate annuity is producing $750 thousand per year—$500 thousand more than your municipal bonds earned. If you were to use $200 thousand to purchase insurance on you and your spouse for your children's benefit, they would receive approximately $4 million—$1.7 million more than they would have received after your $5 million in municipal bonds were subjected to 55% estate taxes of $2.7 million.

If you were to then use an additional $200 thousand per year to purchase a seven pay insurance policy on your children for the benefit of your grandchildren, that $200 thousand could ultimately produce approximately $35 million for your grandchildren!

You would still be receiving $350 thousand per year in income—$100 thousand more than your municipal bonds were producing—your children would receive $1.7 million more than they would have otherwise inherited and your grandchildren receive up to $35 million that did not exist at all.

If you are concerned about releasing the full principal amount, there are other ways to work the same program so that you only use a portion of the full principal to produce the income and insurance premiums. It would only take $1.5 million in immediate annuities to produce the same $250 thousand which is produced by $5 million in municipal bonds. That would leave $3.5 million in bonds and principal. Another $600 thousand invested in immediate annuities would be all it would take to produce the $115 thousand needed to fund the $2.7 million insurance policy for your children. Therefore, $2.1 million in immediate annuities does the work of $5 million in municipal bonds leaving $2.9 million in accessible principal in case of emergency. And, of course, that $2.9 million is still producing 5% income of $145 thousand which can be used to optimize your assets further or simply to enhance your lifestyle.

MUNICIPAL BONDS HAVE NO RESPECT FOR AGE

AAA rated Municipal Bonds pay only 5% whether you are age 30 or 85. Certificates of Deposit - Treasury Bills - Savings Accounts etc. pay less than 5% after tax.

Guaranteed Yearly Return

MALE - $100,000 ANNUITY				
Age	Yield	Return	Tax	Net
60	9.2%	$9,279	$2,078	$7,201
65	10.2%	$10,228	$2,086	$8,142
70	11.6%	$11,678	$2,195	$9,483
75	13.4%	$13,415	$2,200	$11,215
80	16.1%	$16,145	$2,389	$13,756
85	19.9%	$19,965	$2,395	$17,570

FEMALE - $100,000 ANNUITY				
Age	Yield	Return	Tax	Net
60	8.5%	$8,589	$1,752	$6,837
65	9.2%	$9,280	$1,707	$7,573
70	10.1%	$10,173	$1,546	$8,627
75	11.5%	$11,553	$1,386	$10,167
80	13.5%	$13,529	$1,244	$12,285
85	16.7%	$16,749	$1,005	$15,744

WARNING - This plan will reduce your liquidity. Your principal is no longer available. Principal can be replaced on a tax free basis. Taxes calculated above based on a 40% tax bracket and life expectancy.

WHY SETTLE FOR 5%?

All figures are based on current assumptions. Charts are for illustrative purposes only.

©1994 WEALTH CREATION CENTERS℠ - Barry Kaye Associates

15

Make Municipal Bond Money Estate Tax Free

MOST PEOPLE THINK of municipal bonds as tax free investments. But they're not. They're still subject to the same estate taxes as any other investment, asset or liquid resource. And those estate taxes effectively devalue the bonds up to 55%!

Of course, municipal bonds do provide a good source of revenue income tax free. But what if there were a way to retain the full income tax free potential of your municipal bonds while avoiding the necessity for estate taxes so you could pass the full value of the asset on to your heirs? And what if the same plan could be applied to any other investment vehicle such as CD's, T-Bills, Governments, etc., that yields less than 5% net after taxes? Wouldn't you be interested? Well, there is.

To fully understand this remarkable approach, consider the following assumptions: You are 75 . . . your net worth is $5 million . . . you're in the 40% income tax bracket . . . you have invested $1 million in municipal bonds . . . you're receiving a return of 5% over the next 15 years.

On the positive side, your investment will save you $300 thousand on your income taxes over the next 15 years. At a 5% return, the $1 million in bonds earns $50 thousand per year. Given your 40% tax bracket, yearly income taxes on that $50 thousand would have been $20 thousand. Fifteen years of paying $20 thousand in income tax would come to a total of $300 thousand. So you've saved $300 thousand.

But, on the negative side, upon your death, your heirs will owe $550 thousand in estate taxes on that $1 million principal! Almost twice the income tax savings will vanish into the federal government's hands, the same federal government that so generously allowed you to save $300 thousand in income taxes.

There is a better way.

By purchasing an immediate annuity, you could, at age 75, receive approximately $100 thousand annually after income taxes. You would retain the same $50 thousand a year in income which your bonds were producing, but would have an additional $50 thousand remaining from the $100 thousand total. At age 75, you could purchase approximately $2 million of life insurance. By transferring the $50 thousand annually to an irrevocable trust for the benefit of your children or grandchildren, you could arrange for the $2 million in death proceeds to come to them both income and estate tax free.

Though you forfeit the entire principal when you purchase an immediate annuity, you would still receive, each year for the rest of your life, the same income as your municipal bonds produced *plus* your heirs would receive the $2 million in insurance benefits. *You would have truly optimized both your annual income and the inheritance your children receive at no additional outlay whatsoever.*

By "fine tuning" this approach, you can, of course, produce more income for you with less death benefit for your heirs or vice versa, whichever your individual situation requires. But you must remember that, once the immediate annuity is purchased, you can never recover the principal. Sound judgement must be exercised so that your portfolio is properly diversified and only the amount of principal which you can safely and comfortably reallocate is utilized. It would be wise to retain some of your municipal bonds and other fixed assets for any emergency purpose that might arise.

MUNICIPAL BOND ALTERNATIVE

Based on Female - Age 75 - December 17, 1993

	Muni Bond	Increased Income	Increased Inheritance	Maximum Inheritance
Outlay	$1,000,000	$1,000,000	$1,000,000	$1,000,000
Coupon Rate	5%	11%	10.82%	10.62%
Yearly Income	$50,000	$109,973	$108,204	$106,151
Income Tax	$0	($11,085)	($10,907)	($10,700)
After Tax	$50,000	$98,888	$97,297	$95,451
Insurance Premium	$0	($12,994)	($28,875)	($45,451)
Net Income	$50,000	$85,894	$68,422	$50,000
Net Return	5%	8.59%	6.84%	5%
Estate Tax	($550,000)	$0	$0	$0
Net to Family	$450,000	$450,000	$1,000,000	$1,574,064

Increase your income from 5% to 6.84% or 8.59%
from $50,000 to $68,422 or $85,894 - Tax free!

Increase your family's inheritance from $450,000 to $1,000,000 or
$1,574,064 at no additional cost to you!

All figures are based on current assumptions, current taxes and life expectancy. Charts are for illustrative purposes only.

©1994 WEALTH CREATION CENTERS℠ - Barry Kaye Associates

MUNICIPAL BOND ALTERNATIVE

Based on Male/Female - Age 80 - December 17, 1993

	Muni Bond	Increased Income	Increased Inheritance	Maximum Inheritance
Outlay	$1,000,000	$1,000,000	$1,000,000	$1,000,000
Coupon Rate	5%	11.7%	10.98%	10.78%
Yearly Income	$50,000	$111,658	$109,839	$107,772
Income Tax	$0	($12,550)	($12,346)	($12,114)
After Tax	$50,000	$99,108	$97,493	$95,659
Insurance Premium	$0	($13,153)	($29,229)	($45,659)
Net Income	$50,000	$85,955	$68,264	$50,000
Net Return	5%	8.6%	6.83%	5%
Estate Tax	($550,000)	$0	$0	$0
Net to Family	$450,000	$450,000	$1,000,000	$1,562,104

Increase your income from 5% to 6.83% or 8.6%, from $50,000 to $68,264 or $85,955 - Tax free!

Increase your family's inheritance from $450,000 to $1,000,000 or $1,562,104 at no additional cost to you!

All figures are based on current assumptions, current taxes and life expectancy. Charts are for illustrative purposes only.

©1994 WEALTH CREATION CENTERS℠ - Barry Kaye Associates

MUNICIPAL BOND ALTERNATIVE

Based on Male - Age 85 - December 17, 1993

	Muni Bond	Increased Income	Increased Inheritance	Maximum Inheritance
Outlay	$1,000,000	$1,000,000	$1,000,000	$1,000,000
Coupon Rate	5%	19.78%	18.62%	18.28%
Yearly Income	$50,000	$197,775	$186,200	$182,815
Income Tax	$0	($19,461)	($18,322)	($17,989)
After Tax	$50,000	$178,314	$167,878	$164,826
Insurance Premium	$0	($45,695)	($101,545)	($114,826)
Net Income	$50,000	$132,619	$66,333	$50,000
Net Return	5%	13.26%	6.63%	5%
Estate Tax	($550,000)	$0	$0	$0
Net to Family	$450,000	$450,000	$1,000,000	$1,130,792

Increase your income from 5% to 6.63% or 13.26%, from $50,000 to $66,333 or $132,619 - Tax free!

Increase your family's inheritance from $450,000 to $1,000,000 or $1,130,792 at no additional cost to you!

All figures are based on current assumptions, current taxes and life expectancy. Charts are for illustrative purposes only.

©1994 WEALTH CREATION CENTERS℠ - Barry Kaye Associates

16

Create Money to Support Real Estate, Heirs, or Charity by Releasing Principal and Producing Larger Income

THERE ARE REALLY ONLY TWO THINGS that count in later life other than health, family, love and relationships and they are income for you and assets for your heirs. At some age, your thoughts turn to wanting to leave certain assets as a legacy of your love and that becomes of paramount importance. You no longer wish to speculate, you're not playing any more "investment games" and you are beyond the chase. At this point, you simply desire to maximize what you will have to leave to your family. However, the most important thing in your life is income to support your lifestyle—your standard of living. It is such a shame that this is realized so little by most people. They fail to analyze whether they are receiving the maximum amount of income without risk while optimizing what they leave their family.

There are so many instances where assets are held that produce very little income and yet have no opportunity of real appreciation considering estate taxes. Yet, people continue to hold these low paying income stocks and bonds and this effectively non-growth asset. If an asset is to grow substantially only to be reduced by 55% estate taxes at death, it would be better to look at what methods might be utilized to produce at death the maximum amount of money. Only a life insurance product produces this end result since only a life insurance policy pays off with no time element involved. Life insurance will produce the end result you desire whether you die tomorrow, 5 years from now or 25 years from now. It stands alone in delivering the optimum return at your guaranteed death.

Wouldn't it be smarter to utilize immediate annuities to produce, on a guaranteed basis, maximum income for the rest of your life while your irrevocable trust holds insurance policies that will produce maximum assets at the time of your death. However, this should not be done at the expense of liquidity. Both an immediate annuity and life insurance policy reduce your liquidity and no financial tool should be used, no matter how greatly it optimizes your children's inheritance, at the expense of your own lifestyle. Once again, if any investment in an insurance policy or an annuity does not change your lifestyle and does not eliminate your liquidity to a point that is unacceptable to you, why wouldn't you utilize these products?

This sample demonstrates the benefits of immediate annuities, using the example of a man who has a portfolio of approximately $20 million in various real estate properties. He is using the proceeds and equity available from profitable ventures to cover the expenses of some bad deals and is rapidly approaching a point where he is in danger of losing both. He requires an additional $5 million in order to resolve the situation.

Aside from the real estate, the man has only one other major asset: $10 million in municipal bonds which he and his wife had agreed never to sell since it produced the $500 thousand in annual income which supported their lifestyle.

By using an immediate annuity, this man can actually increase his yearly income, provide his children with the same total inheritance and free up the needed $5 million to salvage his real estate deals.

Based on the average age of the man and his wife, an immediate annuity will produce an approximate 12% return after minimal income taxes. Therefore, a $4 million annuity will earn $500 thousand per year. Though the principal will be gone following the death of the man and his wife, they will receive $500 thousand yearly—the same as their $10 million in bonds are currently producing—for the rest of their lives. And this is accomplished using only $4 million of the $10 million total in bonds.

Using $1 million of the remaining $6 million, the man can purchase a life insurance policy which will provide his children with $4.5 million income and estate tax free following the death of their parents. This is the same amount they would have received otherwise since the man's $10 million in "tax free" municipal bonds would still have been subject to estate taxes of 55% or $5.5 million.

In this way, the man and his wife receive the same income and the children's inheritance is fully protected while the remaining $5 million of the original $10 million in bonds can be used to protect the $20 million in real estate investments. Now the children will almost certainly be even more secure as they stand to inherit $20 million worth of viable property holdings which previously were threatened by foreclosure for lack of ample funds to support them.

You can use these same optimizing concepts extremely effectively to release unneeded principal from low-producing assets or to generate and create significantly enhanced income. That released principal can then be used to support family needs, help a brother, start a son in business, make charitable donations, fund educational costs, etc., during your lifetime.

However, *it is important to note that these programs are really only available at older ages.* Since the principal is "used up" in producing the much higher return an immediate annuity yields, the increased rates paid can only be interesting at older ages. There are other means of creating needed assets for younger people many of which are detailed in other sample programs contained within these pages.

CREATE $5 MILLION AT NO COST

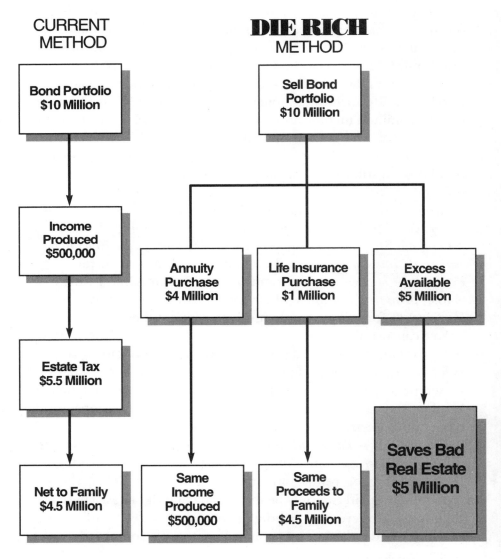

All figures are based on current assumptions. Charts are for illustrative purposes only.

©1994 WEALTH CREATION CENTERS℠ - Barry Kaye Associates

17

Turn $250 Thousand Into $10 Million . . . And More!

THIS CONCEPT OFFERS one of the most dramatic examples of how the programs detailed in this book can make your money work for you in never-before-imagined ways; of how easy it is to optimize your assets and put them to work earning remarkable returns in financial security for generations of your loved ones to come.

For this example, imagine a couple with an average age of 60 (which would earn them a 10–1 return on their last-to-die life insurance investment) who are worth enough that they have an available $1.5 million of "junk" money on the "bottom of their pile."

If they do not take advantage of the concepts presented here, that couple's children will pay $750 thousand in estate taxes on the "extra" $1.5 million upon their parents' deaths. The children will then be left with $750 thousand.

But there are many better ways that the parents could allocate that same $1.5 million and every one of them increases the amount their children will inherit at no additional cost!

The first thing the parents could do is gift their children with the $1 million while they're still alive. Though they would pay $500 thousand in gift taxes [assuming they have already used up their combined $1.2 million Unified Estate and Gift Tax Credit (exemption)], the children would receive $250 thousand more than if the parents held the funds in their estate where the full $1.5 million would be subject to estate taxes. Since this was an excess $1.5 million anyway, it should not hurt the parents to make the gift while they are still alive. In fact, there would probably be some added pleasure in being there to receive their children's appreciation and to help them make the best decisions for how to spend or invest it.

By simply reallocating their available funds the parents have provided their children with 33% more money. But, if they utilize life insurance and an irrevocable trust along with that reallocation, they can increase their children's inheritance more than 400%!

Without any reallocation, at death the children and grandchildren would have received $750 thousand after paying estate taxes of $750 thousand. In giving the gift of $1 million now, they would have received $1 million. But, there is a way for them to ultimately receive up to $12 million at no additional cost!

Working with the same total of $1 million to be gifted to the children now, the parents give them $750 thousand directly and transfer the remaining $250 thousand to an irrevocable trust. The trust then buys a life insurance policy which will yield $2.5 million to the children upon their parents' deaths. Instead of only receiving $750 thousand as in the original way, or even $1 million as in the first example of reallocation, the children now receive $3.25 million—$750 thousand as a gift now plus $2.5 million from the insurance at death. *Their total inheritance from the same base $1.5 million has been increased more than 4 times!*

But what about the grandchildren? Perhaps the couple would like to be certain that their financial security is insured as well. If so, it is an extremely simple goal to accomplish.

Instead of using the whole $250 thousand to purchase insurance on behalf of their children, the couple could split it into two lots of $125 thousand each. Within the irrevocable trust, one $125 thousand policy could be purchased on behalf of the children and another could be purchased on behalf of the grandchildren. Each policy would yield $1.25 million and both generations would be protected from estate taxation. The children are still far better off than they would have been originally. Instead of receiving $750 thousand from the $1.5 million "junk money" they will get $750 thousand now and $1.25 million upon their parents' deaths for a total of $2 million. And the grandchildren will get $1.25 million as well.

This plan can be optimized even further and in such a way that the same $1.5 million which once would have yielded only $750 thousand can now yield $8.25 million!

Instead of using one $125 thousand portion to purchase a policy on themselves for their grandchildren, the couple can use that sum to purchase a policy on their children's lives for their grandchildren's ultimate benefit. Since the children are so much younger, they can receive a policy return of 40 or 50 to 1. Now, when the couple dies their children receive the same $2 million ($750 gifted directly and $1.25 million from the insurance). And, when the couple's children die, the grandchildren receive $6.25 million from the insurance. *Together, the two generations have received $8.25 million from the same $1.5 million which once was going to produce only $750 thousand.*

Lastly, there is a way to realize an almost 20 times greater return on the $1.5 million bringing its total value up to over $12 million!

In the original model the children would receive $750 thousand from the $1.5 million in discretionary funds. But we can assume that if the couple has $1.5 million excess, they must be worth considerably more than that and the children will benefit from other sources of inheritance. The couple could, therefore, leave their children only $750 thousand from the $1.5 million and still provide for their welfare. *The entire remaining $250 thousand could then be used to purchase a life insurance policy on the couple's children for the benefit of their grandchildren. At a projected 50–1 return, the grandchildren would receive $12.5 million at their parents' deaths!*

Using the simple principals of reallocation coupled with the incredible leverage of life insurance, the couple has created a $13.25 million multigenerational legacy by utilizing $1.5 million of "junk" money for the ultimate gift. $13.25 million or $750 thousand—which would you prefer?

$750,000 OR $13,250,000?

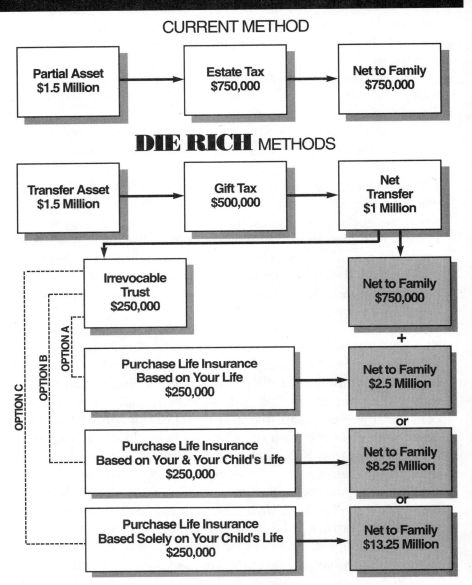

CURRENT METHOD

| Partial Asset $1.5 Million | → | Estate Tax $750,000 | → | Net to Family $750,000 |

DIE RICH METHODS

| Transfer Asset $1.5 Million | → | Gift Tax $500,000 | → | Net Transfer $1 Million |

OPTION A / OPTION B / OPTION C

Irrevocable Trust $250,000 → Net to Family $750,000

+

Purchase Life Insurance Based on Your Life $250,000 → Net to Family $2.5 Million

or

Purchase Life Insurance Based on Your & Your Child's Life $250,000 → Net to Family $8.25 Million

or

Purchase Life Insurance Based Solely on Your Child's Life $250,000 → Net to Family $13.25 Million

All figures are based on current assumptions. Charts are for illustrative purposes only.

18

Multiply Annual Tax Free Gifts 100 Times

WHY WOULD YOU GIVE your child $10 thousand when you could give $1 *million* at no additional cost to you?

You are permitted to gift anyone and everyone you choose with $10 thousand a year without paying any gift or transfer tax. And, if you have a spouse, that spouse may gift anyone with the same $10 thousand a year, also tax free. That means that together, you and your spouse may gift up to $20 thousand a year.

Most financial advisors advise making these yearly gifts, if you can afford to do so. By giving away the money while you're alive rather than waiting for your children to inherit it after you're gone, it removes the principal from your estate and avoids estate taxes. Assuming you are in a 50% estate tax bracket, this saves your children $5–$10 thousand for every year you and your spouse present them with your $10 thousand gifts. If you were to present these gifts every year for ten years, your children would save $50–$100 thousand in estate taxes!

Using the principals detailed in this book, you can increase your children's annual gifts a hundredfold—from $10 thousand to $1 million!

If, instead of giving the $10 thousand to your child directly, you were to place the gift in an irrevocable trust and use it to purchase a last-to-die insurance policy, upon your deaths your child would receive three, five or ten times the amount you had gifted. Plus, he or she would save up to 55% in estate taxes on the principal you had transferred increasing its value even more.

There are many ways to use this program to increase your children's inheritance. Depending on your age and financial situation, you could multiply this program many, many times.

If you and your wife are average age 60 and can afford to gift each child with a combined $20 thousand per year, it could produce at your death, up to $2 million. At average age 70, the yearly $20 thousand payments could produce $1 million and at average age 80 it would produce $700 thousand.

Unless you or your children need the yearly $10 thousand to live on, there is nothing better you could do with it than to use it to purchase a lifetime of financial security for your heirs. If you're already giving the $10 thousand yearly to your children and the money is committed to help with their schooling, medical needs, vacation, etc., you can still gift the additional $10 thousand needed to implement this program though you will have to pay gift taxes of $5 thousand. In this case, you'll be producing the $1 million in benefits from $15 thousand per year. Still a highly optimized program!

The same principal applies to optimizing your one time $600 thousand Unified Estate and Gift Tax credit.

Rather than passing $600 thousand to your heirs at death, you can, using the remarkable potential of life insurance, ultimately leave them $6 million!

If you are financially secure enough that you can afford to transfer $600 thousand to your heirs now rather than holding it within your estate and having your heirs utilize the exemption upon your death, you can place the entire $600 thousand amount into an irrevocable trust without paying any gift or transfer tax. The trust will then purchase a life insurance policy worth $1.8 million if you and your spouse are average age 80, $3 million if you're average age 70, and $6 million if you're average age 60. *Your discretionary $600 thousand multiplies in value up to 10 times!*

TURN $10,000 INTO $1,000,000

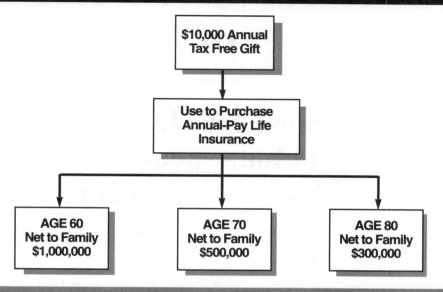

```
           ┌─────────────────┐
           │ $10,000 Annual  │
           │ Tax Free Gift   │
           └────────┬────────┘
                    │
           ┌────────▼────────┐
           │ Use to Purchase │
           │ Annual-Pay Life │
           │   Insurance     │
           └────────┬────────┘
```

| AGE 60 Net to Family $1,000,000 | AGE 70 Net to Family $500,000 | AGE 80 Net to Family $300,000 |

INCREASE YOUR $600,000 EXEMPTION

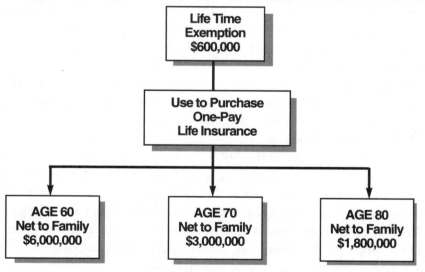

```
           ┌─────────────────┐
           │   Life Time     │
           │   Exemption     │
           │    $600,000     │
           └────────┬────────┘
                    │
           ┌────────▼────────┐
           │ Use to Purchase │
           │    One-Pay      │
           │  Life Insurance │
           └────────┬────────┘
```

| AGE 60 Net to Family $6,000,000 | AGE 70 Net to Family $3,000,000 | AGE 80 Net to Family $1,800,000 |

All figures are based on current assumptions. Charts are for illustrative purposes only.

19

Increase Your Income to Your Spouse 6 Times at Your Death

Many of the concepts which we have presented here revolve primarily around using irrevocable trusts and life insurance to protect your estate value for the benefit of your heirs. *But these same methods can also be utilized to provide greater income and financial security for your spouse.*

Remember, it is your choice whether you transfer your $600 thousand Unified Estate and Gift Tax Credit during your lifetime or at your death. In either case, there is no gift or transfer tax paid upon this $600 thousand.

If you wait to transfer the $600 thousand until your death, your spouse can receive it within a trust from which he/she will be entitled to the earned interest. The $600 thousand could be transferred at your death into a trust for your children because if it goes directly to your spouse it will become a part of his/her estate. Then, when your spouse dies, your children will only benefit from his/her single $600 thousand exemption.

Assuming a yearly interest rate of 5%, the $600 thousand will produce $30 thousand in income.

But, if you can afford to transfer the $600 thousand while you are still alive, you can optimize its value to your spouse up to 6 times!

By transferring the $600 thousand to a trust and purchasing an insurance policy on your life, you can produce up to $3.6 million which will provide income for your spouse upon your death of approximately $180 thousand per year.

You can also use these methods to "buy" the $600 thousand exemption at a greatly reduced cost.

What happens if you want to utilize a liquid $600 thousand to invest in real estate or other financial vehicle, or, you simply do not have $600 thousand, but still want to take advantage of the Unified Estate and Gift Tax Credit for the benefit of your spouse and heirs? If you are male, age 60, and can afford $103 thousand, you can gift it to the trust and use it to purchase a one-pay insurance policy which would produce the full $600 thousand. Your wife would realize the full $600 thousand exemption at a cost of only $103 thousand—an 83% discount. There would still be $497 thousand return for the trust to use in making other investments. If you are a female, age 55, the cost for the insurance would be $63 thousand producing an 89% return and leaving $537 thousand for the trust to invest on your husband's behalf.

$30,000 OR $180,000 YEARLY INCOME FOR YOUR SPOUSE

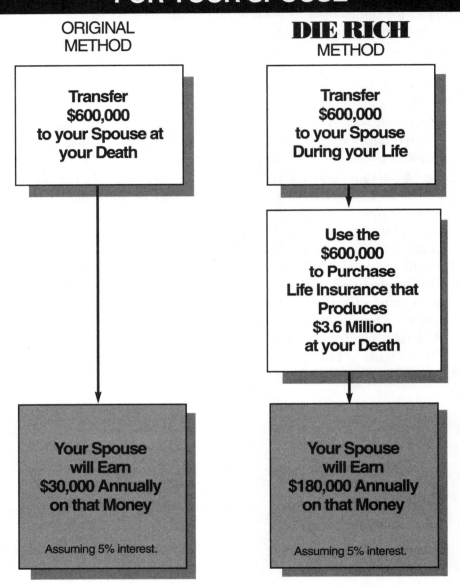

ORIGINAL METHOD

DIE RICH METHOD

**Transfer
$600,000
to your Spouse at
your Death**

**Transfer
$600,000
to your Spouse
During your Life**

**Use the
$600,000
to Purchase
Life Insurance that
Produces
$3.6 Million
at your Death**

**Your Spouse
will Earn
$30,000 Annually
on that Money**

Assuming 5% interest.

**Your Spouse
will Earn
$180,000 Annually
on that Money**

Assuming 5% interest.

All figures are based on current assumptions. Charts are for illustrative purposes only.
This illustration used an insurance policy for a male age 60.
©1994 WEALTH CREATION CENTERS℠ - Barry Kaye Associates

20

Increase the Value of Your Art 4 Times

THE VALUE OF SOME COLLECTIONS or collectibles does not lie within their being part of a set. While collections of coins, stamps, and other items may have to remain grouped as a unit in order to realize their full financial value, other assets such as artwork, rare books, etc., may each have their own separate, intrinsic value. In this case, it is possible that one piece within a collection can be of sufficient value to protect all the others—and the rest of the estate as well. And without that protection, all the pieces are worth only half of their market value to your heirs. Wouldn't it be better to use one piece to protect the remaining ones than to risk having your family have to sell them all in order to pay estate taxes?

Look at an example of a couple with an estate worth $30 million whose heirs would eventually have to pay $16.5 million in estate taxes. Included in the estate is a collection of paintings—16 in all—one of which is worth $5 million. That $5 million piece of art will be worth only $2.5 million to the couple's children and their $30 million estate will be worth only $13.5 million if nothing is done to avoid the loss.

Selling the one $5 million painting now can protect the entire estate for the future which is sure to come.

At approximate average age 80, the couple can receive a little more than a 3–1 return on their insurance investment, based on current assumptions. Selling the painting now for $5 million will purchase a last-to-die policy which will produce the entire $16.5 million estate tax cost following the second death. Not only will they have covered the estate taxes, but they will have avoided the need for forced liquidation which could so tragically devalue their remaining artwork and remove the beloved collection from their children's legacy.

In effect, the couple's $5 million painting—which would have been worth only $2.5 million upon their deaths—has become worth $16.5 million! They have one less painting hanging on the wall, but, in its place, they can hang an insurance document which guarantees their children's future and protects the rest of the collection. Not a bad trade.

Though it may be hard to part with any one piece in a collection you have amassed, wouldn't it be harder still to know that the entire collection might have to be liquidated and lost to your family? You can use your art to provide financial security for your children—and what could be more beautiful than that!

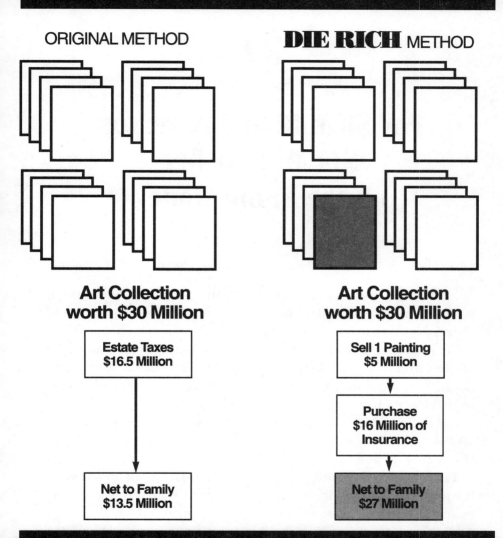

INCREASE THE VALUE OF ONE PAINTING 4 TIMES!

ORIGINAL METHOD

DIE RICH METHOD

Art Collection worth $30 Million

Art Collection worth $30 Million

Estate Taxes
$16.5 Million

Sell 1 Painting
$5 Million

↓

Purchase
$16 Million of
Insurance

↓

Net to Family
$13.5 Million

Net to Family
$27 Million

DOUBLE THE VALUE OF YOUR ART

All figures are based on current assumptions. Charts are for illustrative purposes only.
This illustration used a last-to-die insurance policy for a male and female both age 80.
©1994 WEALTH CREATION CENTERS℠ - Barry Kaye Associates

21

Pay $8 Million Tax Versus $14 Million Tax on the Same Money

Would you pay $14 million in estate taxes on a $24 million estate leaving only $10 million for your children if you could simply and legally pay only $8 million and leave them $16 million? Of course you wouldn't. No one smart enough to amass $24 million would. Or so you would think. But many smart people do because they fail to utilize some simple principals of reallocation in making their estate protection plans.

It doesn't matter if your estate is worth $2.4 million, $24 million, $240 million or $2.4 billion—the means exists for you to provide 60% more money for your children.

This concept does not require the establishment of an irrevocable trust nor the purchase of a life insurance policy. It is a concise example of what creative financial thinking can effect. Simply by reallocating your funds while you are alive you can achieve the promised savings.

If it is your intention to gift your children with your $24 million estate, you have a choice of doing so while you are alive or at your death. If you give it to them while you are alive, you will have to pay a gift tax. If you wait for them to inherit the money at your death, they will pay estate tax. By applying simple arithmetic principles to the situation you will see that gifting them money during your lifetime will increase its net value by 60%.

If your children inherit the $24 million at your death, estate taxes of 55% will claim approximately $14 million.

But, you could gift your children with $16 million now. You will have to pay gift taxes on the transfer of funds of probably 55%. But 55% of $16 million is still only $8.8 million. Since you have removed the money from your estate, at your death there will be no estate taxes to be paid on it. You will have saved $6 million which your children can share and enjoy.

Obviously you can not do this unless you have a means of supporting yourself without the transferred assets. But the point is that gift and estate tax percentages are the same. However, by giving the gift while you are alive, you remove both the principal and the gift tax paid from your estate.

There is no gimmick, no trick. This inarguable reallocation and transfer maneuver will net a 60% increase in your principal's value to your children. You could then use a portion of the $16 million in the trust to purchase life insurance and possibly increase the inheritance up to tenfold and, with a dynasty generation skipping trust, possibly eliminate all estate taxes for the next 100 years!

Gift tax or estate tax . . . in theory they are the same but, as you can see from this example, in practice one can be much more effective than the other when utilized in a considered program of asset reallocation.

THE MORE YOU GIFT THE LESS TAX YOU PAY

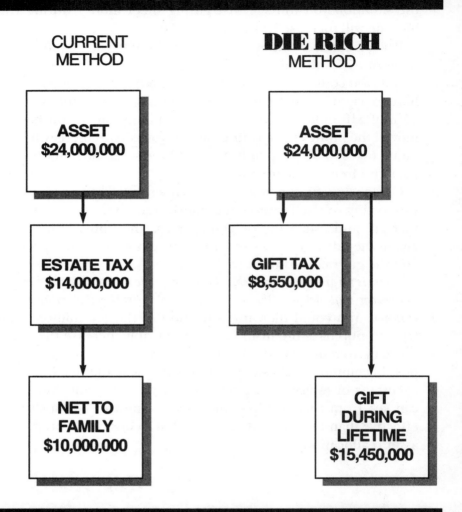

CURRENT METHOD

DIE RICH METHOD

ASSET
$24,000,000

ASSET
$24,000,000

ESTATE TAX
$14,000,000

GIFT TAX
$8,550,000

NET TO FAMILY
$10,000,000

GIFT DURING LIFETIME
$15,450,000

WHY PAY $14 MILLION WHEN YOU CAN PAY ONLY $8,550,000?

All figures are based on current assumptions. Charts are for illustrative purposes only.

22

Avoid All Capital Gains Tax— The Amazing Charitable Remainder Trust

How would you like to avoid all capital gains tax on appreciated property, eliminate your estate tax, receive a stepped up basis in your lifetime, receive 50% more income during your lifetime and increase what you leave your children 4 times while giving substantial gifts to charity, at no cost to you?

This sample program will show you how, once again, using a simple reallocation of assets.

Assume you have appreciated property worth $3 million which you have discounted to a zero cost basis. Capital gains taxes on the $3 million from the sale of the property are $1 million leaving a net asset of $2 million. That $2 million will produce $140 thousand income from a yearly 7%* investment return for you and your spouse as long as either of you is alive. The gross estate your heirs will inherit is $2 million which, because of your other assets, will be subject to estate taxes of $1.1 million leaving your heirs $900 thousand after taxes.

Using a Charitable Remainder Trust, you can put the same $3 million asset to work for you in such a way that:

* Depending on returns and yields at that time.

· You receive a stepped-up basis during your lifetime
· You pay no capital gains taxes
· Your heirs pay no estate tax
· You earn 50% more income
· You leave 400% more to your heirs
· You can give $3 million to charity at no effective cost
· You increase the total value of the property from $900 thousand to $7 million with $4 million going to your heirs and $3 million going to charity

To accomplish these amazing results, you gift the appreciated property to a Charitable Remainder Trust which removes the principal from your estate but allows you and your spouse to receive income for as long as one of you is alive. At your death, the charity receives the principal remaining in the trust. The charity sells the property within the trust paying no income tax due to their charitable exemption.

The $3 million principal in the trust produces, at the same 7%, $210 thousand in yearly income as opposed to the $140 thousand it would otherwise have produced, a 50% increase. In addition, you receive a $1 million tax deduction for the gift to charity (you can't take the whole gift as a deduction because the government knows you'll be receiving income and living for some period of years determined in accordance with their actuarial tables.) That $1 million income tax deduction saves you approximately $350 thousand which, at age 60, you use to purchase a $3.5 million last-to-die insurance policy—possibly $7 million at younger ages, $2 million at older ages. Your children inherit that full $3.5 million income and estate tax free instead of the $900 thousand they would otherwise have inherited—almost 400% more.

You can arrange your own UniTrust or Annuity Trust and be your own Trustee. You can even name your own foundation the beneficiary or you can avoid all administration by affiliating with a "Pooled Income Trust" established by many colleges, hospitals and other charitable institutions.

THE AMAZING CHARITABLE REMAINDER TRUST

1. No Estate Tax
2. Stepped Up Basis in Lifetime
3. No Capital Gains Tax - Increase Income 50%
4. 500% Increase to Heirs
5. $3 Million to Charity at No Cost

	WITHOUT CHARITABLE REMAINDER TRUST	WITH CHARITABLE REMAINDER TRUST
Appreciated Property	$3,000,000	$0
Gift to Charity	$0	($3,000,000)
Capital Gains Tax	($1,000,000)	$0
Net Asset	$2,000,000	$0
Income at 7%	$140,000	$210,000
Income Tax Deduction	$0	$1,000,000
Income Tax Savings	$0	$350,000
Buy Insurance with Tax Savings	$0	$5,000,000
Gross Estate to Children	$2,000,000	$5,000,000
Estate Taxes	($1,100,000)	$0
Net to Charity	$0	$3,000,000
Net Estate to Children	$900,000	$5,000,000
Total to Heirs & Charity	$900,000	$8,000,000

All figures are based on current assumptions. Charts are for illustrative purposes only.
This illustration used a last-to-die insurance policy for a male and female both age 55.
©1994 WEALTH CREATION CENTERS℠ - Barry Kaye Associates

23

Section 6166—Finance Your Tax and It Will Cost You Double

THOUGH FEDERAL ESTATE TAX is generally due nine months following the death of the taxpayer, there are limited circumstances where the estate may claim eligibility for payment of the federal estate tax over an extended period of time. Internal Revenue Code Section 6166 provides that if the value of an "interest in a closely held business" which is included in the taxpayer's estate for federal estate tax purposes exceeds 35% of the taxpayer's "adjusted gross estate", the estate may choose to pay part or all of the federal estate tax attributable to the closely held business interest in up to 10 equal installments. In addition, the first of the 10 equal installments may be deferred for a period of up to five years.

During the deferral period, interest must be paid annually on the entire amount of the deferred estate tax. The interest rate is 4% per annum on the estate tax attributable to the first $1 million of qualifying assets. However, in practice, the 4% interest rate is available only as to $153 thousand of tax (the estate tax on $1 million is $345,800, which is reduced by the unified estate and gift tax credit of $192,800). The balance of the unpaid tax bears interest at the rate charged by the IRS for underpayments of tax.

The election for estate tax deferral under Section 6166 must be made no later than the due date for the Federal Estate Tax Return. The election must contain specific information identifying the assets which qualify for the estate tax deferral and must also contain facts forming the basis for the estate's determination that the estate qualifies for the estate tax deferral.

It is important to note that the estate tax deferral under Section 6166 is available *only* for assets which qualify as an "interest in a closely held business." The remainder of the estate tax is due and payable 9 months following the taxpayer's death. In addition, the estate must satisfy the requirement that at least 35% of the estate is comprised of qualifying closely held business interests for any of the estate tax to be deferred. If an estate holds interests in several different closely held businesses, those interests may be aggregated to satisfy the 35% threshold. As a result of the need to demonstrate that an estate possesses qualifying closely held business interests, there have been many rulings issued by the IRS concerning the availability of the estate tax deferral under particular circumstances.

Many of the rulings issued by the IRS have concerned real estate management businesses. The IRS has focussed on the taxpayer's level of personal involvement in the real estate management business. In particular, if the taxpayer was actively involved in the management of the business (i.e., doing more than merely collecting rents, administering mortgages and paying property taxes and bills), the IRS has often found that the requirements of Section 6166 were met. On the other hand, if the estate has been unable to show any level of personal involvement by the taxpayer, the IRS has concluded that the estate is ineligible for the estate tax deferral.

Even though the estate tax deferral under Section 6166 may be available for a particular estate, that election may have little practical value. As noted above, the estate tax liability will continue to bear interest until it is paid in full, which may result in a tremendous reduction in cash flow to the estate. In addition, the estate tax deferral on the qualifying business interests is available only if the qualifying business interests are not disposed of. If 50% or more of the qualifying closely held business interests are sold, transferred, or withdrawn from the business, the entire unpaid balance of the estate tax will become due and payable. Accordingly, the Section 6166 election represents a reasonable alternative to immediate payment of estate tax for estates with qualifying property.

However, the estate will generally be far better off if a cheaper source of funds is available to satisfy the estate tax obligation. The most cost effective source for those funds will typically be a life insurance policy owned by an irrevocable life insurance trust. In this manner, your heirs will have the option of utilizing Section 6166 if it provides additional cash flow for them or the discount of life insurance—the best of both worlds.

24

Avoid Forced Liquidation

YOUR PRICELESS COLLECTIBLES, property, business, investments may well be facing forced liquidation.

No matter what the composition of your estate, nine months after you die, or after the death of your spouse if you utilize the unlimited marital deduction, estate taxes are due on the entire valuation. If there is not sufficient liquidity to pay the taxes, the government will require your heirs to sell real property in a forced liquidation to come up with the necessary estate tax funds.

The devastation of this process can be unbelievable—both financially and emotionally.

If you have spent a lifetime collecting coins, stamps, figurines, art—anything—that collection represents more than just a financial investment. (Although, realistically, your "collectibles" include your CD's, T-bills, Munis, stock holdings and real estate.) It is an expression of your caring and of you. If some portion of it had to be broken up and sold at liquidation to pay estate taxes, your heirs would lose more than money, they would lose a priceless, invaluable part of you. Furthermore, there is the very real possibility that the collection will be greatly devalued if broken up requiring them to possibly sell the whole collection in order to preserve its financial integrity. The money they receive could not possibly compensate for the loss of your achievement and passion.

There is the same risk with any non-liquid asset. Maybe you have spent your lifetime building a successful business which you started as a small entrepreneurial endeavor and "grew" to a significant accomplishment. Again, that business is more than just a money-making device, it is the expression of your life's work and you probably intend for your children to continue its tradition and success. Maybe it was even your father's business before you and, as such, represents a multi-generational legacy. Were they to have to sell the business in order to raise enough funds to pay estate taxes, it would be a dire emotional loss. To have the family business pass to strangers' hands, to sell the legacy you had created for them with your love and time and effort would be a grievous state of affairs.

Furthermore, there is a very real possibility of preventable financial loss.

With the IRS's clock ticking away, your heirs will have a fixed deadline nine months after your death in which to sell the property. They will not be able to hold out for the best or most fair price, they will have to take what they can get. In a situation like our current recessionary economy, that could well mean that your collection or property would be devalued by some staggering amount. Perhaps 30% of its true value. Perhaps even more. And they would still owe up to 55% of the devalued sale price to the government in estate taxes.

If your estate was worth $30 million in real property and it had to be sold at forced liquidation prices in order to pay the estate taxes, your heirs could conceivably receive only $20 million. Estate taxes of 55% would claim another $11 million. Your heirs would have just $9 million left—less than 1/3—to represent the full value of your lifetime's achievement. Two-thirds would be lost forever; $30 million reduced to $9 million, $150 thousand yearly income (based on 5% interest) reduced to $45 thousand.

You could also borrow the money from the government under Internal Revenue Code Section 6166 and pay the estate tax over a 15 year period. But, again, you'd wind up paying, with principal and interest, virtually double your total estate tax liability.

Once again, life insurance provides the only guaranteed means to prevent this devastation.

At 60 years old, a transfer of $1.65 million to an irrevocable trust will purchase $16.5 million of one-pay life insurance, based on current assumptions, for your heirs which they can use to pay the entire 55% estate tax. At age 70, it would cost $2.3 million and at age 80 it would be $5.5 million. Even with gift taxes added to the "cost" of the premium, this is still a superior method of paying the estate taxes; the discount remains substantial. *In all cases, your heirs would be spared the necessity of a forced liquidation and would receive a far greater return.* If you do not have the liquidity to buy the insurance without liquidating some portion of your estate, the policy purchase can be financed over time allowing you to keep your collection intact.

Wouldn't you rather leave your heirs the full $30 million valuation of your estate and spare them the devastating necessity of selling property which is the symbol of your life's devotion?

25

Avoid All Probate—
The Revocable Living Trust

Most of the concepts in this book make use of an irrevocable trust to transfer money out of a person's or couples' estate in order to avoid estate taxation. However, there are many other types of trusts and legal entities which can be effectively used in estate and financial planning. The revocable living trust is one of them and may be considered one of the best basic estate planning tool in existence.

The following "concept" does not include the purchase of life insurance or examine ways to discount estate taxes, optimize investments or leverage pensions or IRA's. It does, however, detail an important estate planning vehicle.

The revocable living trust (or inter vivos trust) is a written document which provides flexible and coordinated management for assets owned by an individual or married couple. The document can be amended or revoked at any time by the person(s) establishing the Trust. The revocable living trust acts as a receptacle for assets owned by the individual or couple establishing the Trust.

There are three parties (or types of parties) in every revocable living trust. The first party is the individual or married couple establishing the Trust. They are typically called the "Trustors" or the "Settlors." The second party is the individual or trust company managing the trust assets. That party is called the "Trustee." The third party is made up of the individual(s) or charity(ies) who will benefit from the Trust (the "beneficiaries"). In the typical situation, the individual who establishes the revocable living trust is also the Trustee and the beneficiary of the Trust during his or her lifetime.

Though the transfer of assets to a revocable living trust may appear to be a mere paper transaction, the transfer has tremendous significance for estate planning purposes. Legal title to the assets of the Trust is no longer held by the Trustor. Rather, the assets are now held by the Trustee of the Trust. Therefore, those assets will not be subject to probate proceedings in the event of the death of the Trustor, and may be administered privately, confidentially and without delay. In contrast, if a Will is used to pass an individual's property at death, probate proceedings generally must be commenced in order to give effect to the terms of the Will.

Probate proceedings vary from state to state. Certain states have changed their probate statutes to streamline the process. However, in general, the probate process takes at least one year to conclude and the legal fees, personal representative's commissions, court costs and other administrative expenses may consume a substantial portion of the decedent's estate. For example, in California the statutory attorneys' fees in a probate matter are set as a percentage of the *gross* value of the estate. The statutory attorneys' fee on a $5 million estate is $61 thousand and the personal representative is entitled to an equal amount. In addition, there may be extraordinary legal fees for such matters as the sale of property, tax planning and litigation. There may also be extraordinary personal representative's fees for such matters as the operation and management of a business. The amount of the extraordinary fees is set by the court. Various surveys have indicated that the total amount of expense in connection with a probate is typically between 4% and 8% of the gross value of the estate's assets. Obviously, if the estate is highly leveraged, the expenses of probate administration may represent a very substantial portion of the equity of the estate.

Probate proceedings are also very public in nature. Inventories of estate assets must be filed with the court, and the provisions for disposition of assets and property contained within the decedent's Will become a matter of public record. Not surprisingly, the news media may find matters of a personal nature to be highly newsworthy. In addition, it may be quite easy for an aggrieved family member or other party to start a Will contest, since the probate proceeding is the proper and convenient legal forum for such matters to be addressed.

The use of a revocable living trust avoids the problems inherent in the probate process, because the assets of the revocable living trust avoid the probate process. In contrast to the cost, delays and publicity found in probate, the administration of a revocable living trust may be accomplished with relatively little expense, minimal delay, and no public disclosures. Though the successor Trustee of the Trust will need to consult with advisors concerning trust administration and the preparation of tax returns (including the federal estate tax return), the legal expense incurred in a living trust-centered estate plan is far less than the legal fees of a probate proceeding.

The use of the revocable living trust will also allow greater continuity of management of assets. This may be of critical importance in continuing to operate a business or professional practice. Since the fair market value of a business enterprise may diminish at an alarming rate following the death of a principal, the continued operation or sale of the business can be accomplished by the successor Trustee, without requiring the commencement of probate proceedings. In some circumstances, it may be advisable to name in the living trust document one or more Special Trustees, who will have the task of managing and operating the business assets. It may also be advisable to name specific individuals to act as Special Trustees to manage the Trust's investment portfolio. These decisions and countless others should be made in advance by the Trustor in consultation with advisors, with a view towards preserving and maintaining the assets of the Trust.

A revocable living trust will also avoid the need to establish probate proceedings in different states upon the death of an individual. The estate of an individual who dies leaving tangible assets in different states may be required to commence probate administration in each of those states, which may necessitate the involvement of many attorneys and result in tremendous administration expenses. In contrast, if the individual used a revocable living trust to hold title to assets in different states, there would be one centralized management system to cover all of those assets.

The use of the revocable living trust may avoid the establishment of legal proceedings for an individual who has become incapacitated or incompetent. This type of proceeding may also be known as a conservatorship or guardianship and is typically very expensive and may be emotionally devastating to the affected individual. If the revocable living trust is properly structured and funded, the assets of the Trust will be available to care for the affected Trustor, without having to commence legal proceedings. Rather, once the individual's attending physicians have certified the individual's incapacity, the successor Trustee will be able to step in and manage the Trust's assets to provide appropriate care for the affected Trustor. Once again, by providing for a prompt succession of Trustees, there need be no gap in the management of Trust assets.

There are very few reasons not to use a revocable living trust. Some people have argued that it is difficult to fund a living trust. Others have suggested that it is not cost effective to use a living trust, since it is typically more expensive to create a living trust than a Will. In fact, the funding of a living trust is crucial to its success and can be accomplished through a number of techniques. The expense involved in creating a living trust is usually not significant, but there is a tremendous payoff from that investment, by avoiding probate and creating a flexible and coordinated management system for assets. There is much to gain and very little to lose by using a revocable living trust as the core document in your estate plan.

26

Beat Any Investment with a 10 to 1 Return

IF YOUR FINANCIAL ADVISOR told you of an investment that would produce a guaranteed return of up to 10 to 1 which you would receive income and estate tax free and which would pay this return from the first day you made the investment, what would you do? The answer is obvious—you'd buy in.

Well, there is such an investment. But your advisors may not be aware of its full potentials or think of it in investment terms.

It is a sound and common financial strategy to multiply principal using investments and then live off the income of those investments keeping the principal intact for future generations or as a protection against some emergency. It is also common knowledge that in order to produce the higher levels of income or realize the higher appreciation on investments, you must be willing to take higher risks.

Many people continue investing, even after they are at a point where their principal produces sufficient income to support their lifestyle, simply to amass a greater legacy for their children. They keep moving their money around looking for the greatest return so they can have more to invest and, hopefully, earn even more so their children will inherit more. *Yet they overlook the one investment guaranteed to provide a significant return and the fact that virtually every other investment they make will be worth only about 30% of whatever profit they earn.*

Even if you or your advisors found an investment that ultimately paid a 10 to 1 return, it would only be worth 66% to 72% after income taxes and then 45% of that after estate taxes. If a $500 thousand investment grossed $5 million, income taxes would take about $1.6 million leaving $3.3 million which would be subject to estate taxes of $1.8 million. The $5 million gross would be reduced to $1.5 million net—less than ⅓ of the original $5 million. If you waited until death and received the full stepped-up basis, therefore avoiding income taxes, it would still be worth only $2.8 million.

In order to realize the full $5 million as a net gain, the investment would have had to increase not 10 times but 30 times—the initial $500 thousand would have to increase to $15 million gross in order to net $5 million if you were to sell now—or at least to $10 million if it is held in your estate and the full stepped-up basis is realized.

But, as you have seen over and over again through the sample programs in this book, the same $500 thousand of initial investment could, through the use of an irrevocable trust and the leverage of life insurance produce a guaranteed net return of $5 million to your heirs, based on current assumptions. You take virtually no risk in making this amazing investment and it will pay the guaranteed return tomorrow if need be.

If your financial strategy is to invest some portion of your principal to produce income to ultimately enlarge your estate for your children's benefit, if you do not need the investment income of that portion of your principal to support your own lifestyle, there is no better investment you could make on behalf of your children's or grandchildren's financial security than an investment in life insurance.

BEAT ANY INVESTMENT

Compare the Difference $1,000,000 Produces After Death*

Asset	1 Year Later	10 Years Later	30 Years Later
Stocks	$540,000	$1,079,463	$5,031,328
Real Estate	$540,000	$1,079,463	$5,031,328
Bonds	$540,000	$1,079,463	$5,031,328
T-Bills	$540,000	$1,079,463	$5,031,328
Art/Antiques	$540,000	$1,079,463	$5,031,328
Last-to-die Insurance	$10,000,000	$10,000,000	$10,000,000

*Based on 8% return and current assumptions after estate taxes. This is a last-to-die life insurance policy in an irrevocable trust. For Male and Female age 60 the program produces $10,000,000; Age 70 produces $5,000,000; Age 80 produces $3,300,000.

THE CHOICE IS YOURS!

All figures are based on current assumptions. Charts are for illustrative purposes only.

27

Buy Insurance Even if You're Uninsurable

Many people who have come to realize the dramatic power of life insurance as part of a diversified portfolio of financial investment are concerned that they will not be able to take advantage of its guaranteed returns and tax free benefits because they are uninsurable. Perhaps they believe they are too ill or too old to realize a cost-effective return. *If you are one of these people, do not despair—there are several ways in which you can participate in the optimizing effects of life insurance to create and preserve wealth.*

The first option you have is to verify whether or not you are truly uninsurable. Different insurance companies use different standards and it is possible that even if you were turned down by one, another will accept you. Additionally, as medical knowledge increases, some conditions which previously were considered too serious to qualify for insurance coverage are now treatable in ways that coverage can be issued. It is important that your insurance advisor be knowledgeable into all the particulars and have access to numerous insurance companies.

The second method which can be utilized is to select a "surrogate insured."

If for some reason neither you or your spouse is a good candidate for insurance coverage, look around at the members of your extended family for someone more suitable to be insured. Perhaps your children have an uncle and/or aunt, a godparent or cousin who is in better health or younger than you are who can serve as the surrogate.

In all likelihood, there is some member of your extended family who would make a good candidate. When you have selected that person who represents the best return on the insurance investment, arrange for them to be examined. You then set up a trust naming your children as trustees and gift the money to the trust on their behalf. There may be some gift taxes but they will still be considerably less than the amount estate taxes would ultimately cost your children. The trust buys the insurance policy on the surrogate earning the appropriate rate depending on their age and health and names the trust as its beneficiary. The insurance proceeds ultimately come to your children gift and estate tax free upon the death of the surrogate replacing any estate tax loss your estate suffered upon your death. If the surrogate happens to die before you do, the policy proceeds will "wait" in the trust to pay the estate taxes due upon your death.

Using this plan, the numbers would work as follows:

You have an estate valued at $50 million and both you and your spouse are uninsurable. Your brother and his wife, who enjoy an average age of 60, *are* insurable and so you select them to be your surrogates.

The estate taxes on your $50 million will be $27.5 million which, without insurance to replace it, your children will lose forever. At their average age of 60, you can purchase on the aunt and uncle a one-pay, last-to-die insurance policy for $2.75 million. You transfer this amount to the trust, paying some gift taxes depending on your previous use of your exemptions. The trust buys the insurance policy which ultimately nets your children $27.5 million completely replacing the amount paid in estate taxes. The total cost of the plan was $2.75 million for the policy and, at most, $1.3 million in gift taxes. *This leaves a substantial $25 million in saved losses for your heirs.*

It is important to note that not all insurance companies accept the surrogate method and the proposal must be presented properly to the ones who have exhibited definite interest.

There is a third method for accomplishing the $27.5 million savings as well, at an even greater discount.

If there isn't anyone who you can use as a surrogate, you may have to face the fact that estate taxes will take $27.5 million from your children's inheritance. *But you can recapture that whole amount for your grandchildren's benefit . . . after all, they are also a cherished extension of you. You can even significantly increase it.*

Even if you are uninsurable, chances are good that your children are insurable. Though they will face the loss of the $27.5 million in estate taxes, if you were to purchase a policy on their lives for the benefit of their children, *you could replace the entire tax in the second generation at $1/40$–$1/50$ of its cost.* At a 50–1 return, based on your grandchildren's parents being average age 40, the entire $27.5 million could be returned to your grandchildren for a one-pay cost of $550 thousand by using an irrevocable trust to purchase last-to-die insurance on their parents for their ultimate benefit.

But you don't have to settle for replacing the lost estate tax cost. If you are concerned about the time period involved in waiting for your children's deaths to replace the estate tax costs levied at your death, you could spend 2 to 3 times as much ($1.1 million to $1.6 million) so your grandchildren would collect up to 2 to 3 times more in insurance benefits—$83 million tax free. This would surely cover any financial loss due to inflation during the time between your death and your children's death. It would also provide funds for your grandchildren to use in paying any estate taxes that may be due upon their parents' assets. Your grandchildren would not only recapture the $27.5 million which your children "lost" to taxes, they could receive an additional $55.5 million!

Any one of these plans will allow those of you who are uninsurable to preserve the wealth you have amassed and even create incredible new wealth for your children and grandchildren at a fraction of the cost of what estate taxes will claim.

SURROGATE INSURED

Uninsurable

Parents

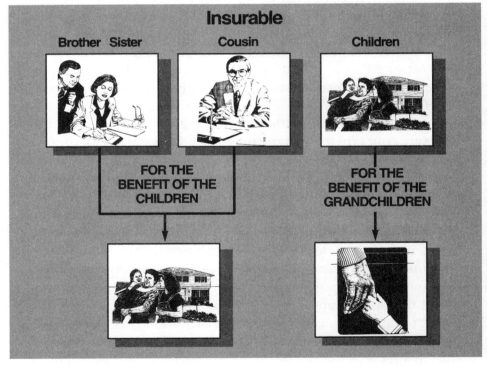

Insurable

Brother Sister	Cousin	Children

FOR THE
BENEFIT OF THE
CHILDREN

FOR THE
BENEFIT OF THE
GRANDCHILDREN

All figures are based on current assumptions. Charts are for illustrative purposes only.

28

Optimize Investment Profits and Principal

You can use the programs described on these pages to increase investment profits three, five, even ten times over.

With interest rates on CD's, money markets, etc., so low, many people are looking into investment vehicles that offer a potential of more substantial returns. But there is one investment opportunity which often gets overlooked—life insurance. Because financial advisors are not used to thinking of life insurance as an investment, these people may be missing out on the best investment strategy there is.

If you use your principal to invest in the stock market, real estate trust deeds, bonds—virtually any financial vehicle—you can use life insurance and an irrevocable trust to leverage the profits you earn income and estate tax free.

In today's world of 5% interest, if that, you'd probably be very happy with any investment that produced 10%. 15% would make you ecstatic. But even doubling or tripling the potential return does not earn near as much as you think it does over the years. Especially if your primary purpose in making the initial investment is to increase your estate for the ultimate benefit of your heirs. Furthermore, any effort toward doubling your investment involves an equal amount of risk. These applications do not apply if you need the income or principal for your own lifestyle.

If you were to invest $5 million and receive a 10% return, you would have earned $500 thousand. Income tax on those earnings would be about $200 thousand leaving $300 thousand which would be subject to estate taxes of $165 thousand. Your heirs would inherit only $135 thousand for each additional year you live if you were to look at those years in isolation. (In actuality, there will be some compounding benefit but, those compounded earnings will also be subject to income and estate taxes, making them worth only a fraction of their original value as well. Your compounding benefits will be decimated at the same percentage as your principal and other earnings.) Ten years of isolated earnings of $135 thousand net after taxes could amount to approximately $1.35 million. Add that to the $2.8 million net after estate taxes on your $5 million principal for a total of $4.1 million. Over twenty years, the interest earnings could come to $3.3 million which, when added to the same $2.8 million net after tax principal, totals $6.1 million.

Even if your $5 million investment earned 15%—$750 thousand—after income taxes of $225 thousand and estate taxes of $288 thousand there would only be $237 thousand left for your heirs. They actually receive less than the 5% gross interest you were dissatisfied with to start.

But, if you were to use the 10% or 15% investment earnings to purchase life insurance within an irrevocable trust, you could increase the return significantly and dramatically reduce the estate tax costs.

If you are average age 60, and you were to transfer the $300 thousand which remained of your 10% investment profit after you'd paid income taxes of $200 thousand in the first year of earnings, it could be used to purchase a policy which, upon the deaths of you and your spouse, would produce $3 million for your heirs. If either one of you had not already used your $600 thousand Unified Estate and Gift Tax Credit, there would be no gift tax on the transfer and the insurance proceeds would come to your heirs estate tax free. *It would take 22 years of receiving a 10% return on*

*your initial $5 million investment (barring compounding) to equal the
$3.5 million return of the insurance policy. Yet the insurance return is
guaranteed from the very first day,* based on current assumptions.
(Refer to chart on page 145).

*More dramatically, if you were to use each year's $300 thousand after
tax earnings to purchase a life-pay policy, it would pay proceeds of $30
million upon your death,* based on current assumptions, though
there would be some gift taxes required to make the yearly transfers after the fourth year. (After the first four years, the total of
your $300 thousand annual transfer would come to $1.2 million
which is the limit of you and your spouse's combined Unified
Estate and Gift Tax Credit Exemption.)

If you and your spouse are average age 70, a single year's $300
thousand would buy $1.5 million—6 times the $237 thousand
your heirs would realize after income and estate taxes were paid
on the original $750 thousand interest earnings. And if you are
average age 80, it will purchase approximately $1 million of insur-
ance representing a 4 times greater return income and estate tax
free using proceeds from one year only. Using the investment
returns each year to purchase life-pay policies, the returns could
be $15 million at average age 70 and $6 million at average age 80.

With a 15% investment return of $750 thousand gross, $525
thousand net after income taxes, you would still pay no transfer
tax assuming you had not already used your $600 thousand ex-
emption. At age 60, the $525 thousand would produce $5.2 million. At age 70, it would earn $2.6 million and at 80 it would
produce $1.5 million.

*Clearly, the tax free, guaranteed return of the life insurance investment
would optimize your investment earnings many times over the best you
could ever hope the market to return.*

But think of this. What if, instead of only optimizing the investment return of your $5 million principal, you were to reinvest the
entire principal amount in a life insurance policy in order to
optimize the full $5 million to the extent that you could secure the
coverage.

At average age 60, $5 million could produce as much as $50

million, based on current assumptions. At average age 70, it could purchase a policy worth $25 million to your heirs and at average age 80 it could return as much as $15 million, based on current assumptions.

If the income and/or principal represents discretionary funds, there is clearly no better way to optimize its value to your heirs than through the purchase of life insurance.

INCREASE INVESTMENT PROFITS 3, 5, EVEN 10 TIMES

If your $5,000,000 investment yields 10%

CURRENT METHOD

| Investment Yields Income $500,000 | → | Income Tax on Investment $200,000 | → | Estate Taxes on Investment $165,000 | → | Net to Family $135,000 |

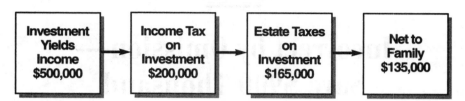

DIE RICH ALTERNATIVE METHODS

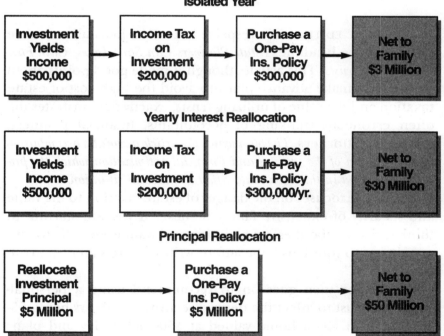

Isolated Year

| Investment Yields Income $500,000 | → | Income Tax on Investment $200,000 | → | Purchase a One-Pay Ins. Policy $300,000 | → | Net to Family $3 Million |

Yearly Interest Reallocation

| Investment Yields Income $500,000 | → | Income Tax on Investment $200,000 | → | Purchase a Life-Pay Ins. Policy $300,000/yr. | → | Net to Family $30 Million |

Principal Reallocation

| Reallocate Investment Principal $5 Million | → | Purchase a One-Pay Ins. Policy $5 Million | → | Net to Family $50 Million |

All figures are based on current assumptions. Charts are for illustrative purposes only.
This illustration used a last-to-die insurance policy for a male and female both age 60.
©1994 WEALTH CREATION CENTERS℠ - Barry Kaye Associates

29

Incorrect by Omission—
Save $900 Thousand

See / 197

IN A RECENT EDITION of a respected financial journal, an article
ran under the headline: *Estate Planners Can Save Taxes, Gain Flexibility With Trusts.* This article, though it made good points about
the need to make advance plans to avoid the high cost of estate
taxation and the value of utilizing trusts, exactly demonstrates the
often erroneous thinking of accountants, financial planners,
writers and attorneys. *The plan which the article advocates accomplishes
only a fraction of the savings and financial optimization which the programs described in this book could affect in the same situation.*

The article focuses on the danger of estate taxation to the value
and security of expensive family homes. "If you are starting to
think seriously about estate planning and want eventually to give
your home to your kids," the author writes, "here's an idea worth
considering."

· The author then goes on to recommend using a personal-
residence trust to affect the desired security. He shows how a 55-
year-old man has a home valued at $500,000 today and plans
ultimately to turn it over to his daughter. But he still would like to
live in the home for another 15 years.

"If the home appreciates at 4% a year, it will be valued at
$900,472 in 15 years. If the man is in the top estate-tax bracket

146

[55%], his daughter would have to pay a combined federal and state estate tax of $495,259 on the home if the man died with the home in his estate", the article quoted a national director of estate planning for a respected accounting firm in Philadelphia.

He further stated, "But if the man placed his home in a personal-residence trust with a 15-year term, his taxable gift to his daughter would be valued at a fraction of its fair market value—at $143,975 today."

The article goes on to explain that the home's current fair-market value is reduced by approximately one-third within the trust because the daughter won't receive it for 15 years. Therefore, the gift taxes due on the transfer of the home to the trust will be based on the $143,975 asset valuation. "The potential estate-tax savings is a stunning $416,073," stated the same financial professional.

There are many drawbacks to this plan, some of which the article describes. Firstly, if the man dies during the 15-year term of the trust, the property reverts to his estate and *virtually no savings are effected.* Secondly, if the man lives longer than the 15 years, his home automatically becomes the property of his daughter and he is required by law to lease it from her at a fair market rental cost if he wants to continue living there without incurring additional gift tax. Thirdly, the daughter will lose all "step up" in the property's cost basis for capital gains tax purposes. For income tax purposes, the home will be valued at the original cost basis of the Grantor when placed into the trust. The gain the daughter realizes over that value and the price it sells for after his death will be fully subject to capital gains taxes. Had the father not placed the home in a personal residence trust, his daughter would have inherited it at its full market value and therefore any profit she made upon its sale would only be calculated over the inheritance value instead of the original value. "Even so, your off-spring is still a clear winner by using a personal-residence trust, says a New York attorney who specializes in estate planning," the article concludes.

This conclusion is distressingly typical of the narrow thinking used by so-called leaders in the estate planning and taxation fields. WHAT THEY

FAIL TO REALIZE IS THAT, USING LIFE INSURANCE AND AN IRREVOCABLE TRUST, THE ESTATE TAX COSTS CAN BE VIRTUALLY ELIMINATED WITHOUT ANY OF THE RISKS OR RESTRICTIONS WHICH THEIR PLAN INCLUDES.

Under the personal residence trust method, gift taxes on the $143,975 value of the home when it was transferred to the daughter would be $79,186, 55% of the total valuation.

The alternative and far superior approach to this problem would be to utilize a one-payment, last-to-die life insurance policy. Based on the average age of 55, the same $79 thousand in taxes that the individual would have to pay using the "personal residence trust" method would purchase a one-payment insurance policy with a death benefit of $1.4 million, based on current assumptions. Obviously, the income and estate tax free return of $1.4 million far surpasses the advantage of saving $416 thousand in taxes. *In this manner, the family could pay the estate taxes of $495 thousand and still have in excess of $900 thousand left over.*

As importantly, using the irrevocable trust method allows the parents to retain their house for their own purposes. They would avoid the emotional distress that could arise from the loss of their home and having to rent it back from their own child. What if difficulties arose with property values and the daughter wanted to sell the property while it was still a marketable asset? What would the parents do then? This home almost surely represents a great emotional investment to the parents. Having to give it up during their lifetimes is a lot to ask—especially when it is so unnecessary! Furthermore, if the parents die within the fifteen year limitation of the personal residence trust, their daughter will be exposed to the entire estate tax as the real estate will go back into their parents' estate.

One final point. If the parents retain their real estate until their death, it will receive a stepped-up basis, and, in this manner, if the house is worth $900 thousand, there will be no income taxes for their children if they choose to sell the house. Using the personal residence trust, if the children choose to sell the house, they will have the cost-basis of the parents, which could be as low as $100 thousand, thus producing a capital gains tax in excess of $240 thousand.

It simply doesn't seem prudent to save $416 thousand and possibly give the government back up to $250 thousand in capital gains taxes, leaving a savings of only $166 thousand, when the same monies could produce $1.4 million—almost ten times as much—of income and estate tax free insurance. Even after paying the $495 thousand of estate taxes, the daughter would realize over $900 thousand, surely better than the $166 thousand she'll have left if she sells the house and pays the capitals gains tax.

There are other situations in which "half-way" solutions such as the one discussed in this newspaper article are recommended where irrevocable trusts and life insurance would reap far better returns.

One particular concept often utilized by attorneys is the method of giving away a person's business or other assets in order to lower the ultimate estate taxes. While this can be appropriate if the asset under consideration is appreciating, *the best method cannot be determined without considering the remarkable leverage life insurance provides.*

If a man has built a business which is currently worth $5 million and is anticipated to appreciate to $10 million, his attorneys may counsel him to transfer the business to his heirs now to save on the ultimate estate taxes. Their reasoning is that the $5 million asset will only cost $2.2 million in gift or transfer taxes if taken out of the estate now as opposed to the approximate $5 million in estate taxes if the heirs inherit an appreciated asset worth $10 million.

However, if the attorneys had properly assessed the value of life insurance, they would have realized that for a cost of only $500 thousand, assuming the man is age 60, a policy could be purchased within an irrevocable trust which would produce $5 million for his heirs that could be used to pay the entire $5 million estate tax if the business had grown to $10 million. Since the man has a $600 thousand Unified Estate and Gift Tax Credit, no gift taxes would be required. *Rather than bearing a $2.2 million transfer cost to protect the ultimate $10 million inheritance, he could have used only $500 thousand to accomplish the same protection and retained ownership* *of the business which may well define his purpose and provide years more of enjoyment and satisfaction.*

Obviously, it is more advantageous to utilize the insurance approach and much less costly, yet, without proper recognition of this fact by expert advisors and with incomplete articles running in the media, many people are following plans which do not fully protect their ultimate best interests and become the sad victims of conventional wisdom.

PAY GIFT TAX OR BUY INSURANCE

	CURRENT METHOD	SUGGESTED METHOD	**DIE RICH** METHOD
Current Market Value	$500,000	$500,000	$500,000
Value of Taxable Gift Personal-residence Trust	$0	$143,975	$0
Gift Tax	$0	*($79,186)	$0
Purchase Insurance	$0	$0	($79,186)
Annual Appreciation	4%	4%	4%
Value 15 years later	$900,472	$900,472	$900,472
Net Asset at Death	$900,472	$821,286	$821,286
Estate Taxes	($495,259)	$0	($451,707)
Capital Gains Tax	$0	$250,000	$0
Insurance Pays	$0	$0	$1,400,000
Net to Family	$405,213	$571,286	$1,769,579
Save	$0	$166,073	$1,364,366

* Gift tax is based on $143,975 taxable value of home given to trust.

THE DIFFERENCE MEANS AN EXTRA $1,364,366 FOR YOUR CHILDREN

All figures are based on current assumptions. Charts are for illustrative purposes only.
This illustration used a last-to-die insurance policy for a male and female both age 55.
©1994 WEALTH CREATION CENTERS℠ - Barry Kaye Associates

30

Amazing Results at Younger Ages— $50.5 Million for $50,000

Many younger people think of life insurance as a necessary evil you buy as protection against some tragic emergency. Because of that thinking, they miss out on some of the best opportunities for wealth creation available today. Additionally, many older people thinking of purchasing insurance on themselves for the sake of their children overlook the fantastic returns available by insuring the lives of their children on behalf of their grandchildren.

At younger ages, the return on a life insurance policy is dramatic. Using the one-pay, five-pay or ten-pay methods recommended here, the costs per return for the policy are optimized, based on current assumptions.

Now is a great time for younger people to take advantage of insurance opportunities. With interest rates low, the assumptions upon which insurance companies base their investment returns are also low. But, should interest rates rise, the insurance company will make a greater return on the money you pay them and this will mean that either the cost of your policy will decrease or the ultimate proceeds it produces will increase. *Current assumptions are at a very favorable level for insurance buyers.*

Given these favorable conditions, young couples can realize returns of 40–50 times! And they can use those returns to provide substantial yearly income for their heirs for many generations to come.

If, at average age 40, you and your spouse were to purchase a life insurance policy for $150 thousand using a one-pay method, you could realize proceeds of up to $7.5 million for your heirs. At your deaths, the $7.5 million can be held by the insurance company thus providing approximately $375 thousand in yearly interest to your heirs, based on a 5% return. This return will be paid yearly, virtually forever, to your heirs and theirs in an estate tax free dynasty trust.

At any time, the Trustee can request the principal insurance amount from the insurance company. They would produce the full $7.5 million benefit. Should assumptions change and interest rates rise, that $7.5 million could be utilized as investment income in other financial vehicles. Of course, one such vehicle could be additional life insurance purchased by your heirs through the irrevocable trust on behalf of their heirs. *In this way, financial security for your family can be guaranteed in perpetuity.*

There are several additional ways in which the dramatic returns available at younger ages can be even more greatly optimized, especially for young people who have already achieved significant financial success.

Consider the following model. You have seen the same principals applied to other situations earlier in this book, but look at what it can do at younger ages.

If a couple, average age 40, were to already have achieved a $20 million estate, perhaps through inheritance or business success, they could easily borrow $1 million for a cost of 5% or $50 thousand per year.

Taking the $1 million, they gift it to charity with $500 thousand being designated for current operating expenses and the additional $500 thousand being used to purchase an insurance policy on their lives. Based on current assumptions, *that $500 thousand could ultimately produce as much as $25 million for the charity!*

In addition, the $1 million gift to charity is completely tax deductible and could expect to produce a $500 thousand tax savings. Using this "found" $500 thousand, the couple purchases another last-to-die policy on themselves for the benefit of their children. It will also return, based on current assumptions, $25 million *making their total insurance benefits, from the same $50 thousand per year interest, $50 million*—$25.5 million for charity and $25 million for their heirs. Capitalizing on their younger ages, the couple will have effectively "borrowed" $50.5 million for only $50 thousand per year.

$50.5 MILLION FOR HEIRS, CHARITY & FOUNDATION FOR $50,000 YEARLY

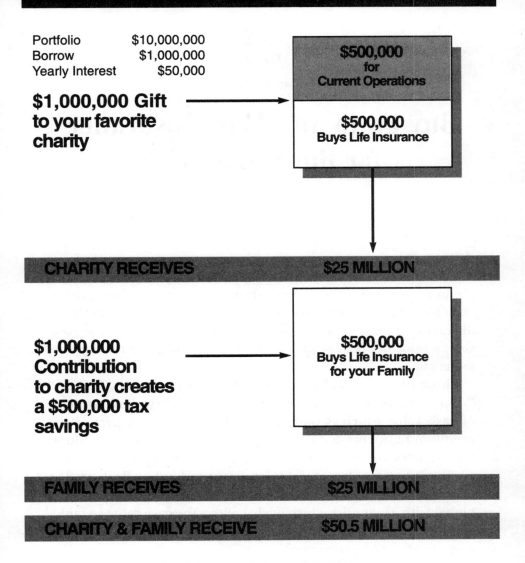

Portfolio	$10,000,000
Borrow	$1,000,000
Yearly Interest	$50,000

$1,000,000 Gift to your favorite charity →

$500,000
for
Current Operations

$500,000
Buys Life Insurance

CHARITY RECEIVES   **$25 MILLION**

$1,000,000 Contribution to charity creates a $500,000 tax savings →

$500,000
Buys Life Insurance for your Family

FAMILY RECEIVES   **$25 MILLION**

CHARITY & FAMILY RECEIVE   **$50.5 MILLION**

Add or remove a zero for larger or smaller estates.

31

Buy Up to 30% More Insurance for the Same Price

THERE ARE NUMEROUS TYPES and varieties of insurance policies available in today's competitive marketplace which offer a plethora of advantages and disadvantages. When utilizing insurance for estate planning purposes, it is important to review these different options. *Depending on the choice you make, the type of policy you purchase can provide up to 30% greater proceeds for the same premium cost.*

Think of two of the basic types of policies as being "fat" and "thin" policies. The terms fat and thin have to do with the amount of cash value which is built up within the policy as part of the premium payments. Fat policies build up substantial cash values; thin policies are structured to avoid paying the higher premiums which cause the policy to yield significant cash value. Both pay the same death benefit, but the cost for the same level of proceeds is higher with a fat policy which is what allows the cash value to build.

Why then, would anyone choose to utilize a fat policy and pay more for the same coverage?

The answer is that at the time you purchase your policy, the premium charged for the desired amount of death benefit is based on the current assumptions of interest and mortality. Should those assumptions change, the cost of the policy would

156

change accordingly. Obviously, a thin policy has more exposure should any of the assumptions change. A fat policy with a larger premium and more cash value will accommodate almost any change in the assumptions to a minor degree without additional premium payments or higher premiums. However, if you utilize a thin policy it will have no tolerance for any change or variance from the original assumptions. If the interest rates stay low and at their current assumption, the policy will last for your entire lifetime, in fact it may well last beyond your assumed life expectancy and on to age 95 to 100. However, if interest should drop below the current rates, you could be required to pay additional premium or the policy would last only to approximately age 92. Each additional drop in the interest can cause this to happen since the insurance company would be losing money—it would not be realizing its projected earning potential which would read on the books as a loss.

Current insurance company interest assumptions are approximately 6% to 7% with many of the policies guaranteed never to be below 4% to 5.5%. This leaves very little room for any kind of a drop that would impact the policy greatly.

On the other hand, if interest should rise, it will increase the amount of cash value, since the insurance company will now be earning more than it had originally projected. This excess could be used to increase the ultimate death benefit or to produce cash in the policy that could be removed or borrowed against.

In other words, should there be an increase in interest rates, a thin policy can become fat while a fat policy could become obese.

Assumptions about mortality—your life expectancy as defined by the insurance company actuarial tables—can also change and impact the cost or value of your policy. However, for the most part mortality has improved over the past decades. People are living longer and new medical discoveries, scientific health maintenance techniques and no smoking habits have produced greater longevity for older people. Nonetheless, the guaranteed rates in any policy relative to mortality can also produce a longer payment schedule or higher premiums.

This is also true with dividend policies where the dividends reflect any change in expense, mortality, and interest.

The basic premise of both policies is that the premium will never go up and the death benefit will never go down. However, the number of years you have to pay for a policy could increase if any of the above changes occur. Yet, even if changes in assumptions were to occur and render your policy of less value or significantly higher cost than you had desired, there are still many options available to you. The policy could be surrendered. The extra years' premium could be paid. The premium could be borrowed against the existing cash value. And one final option is always available: You could reduce the amount of insurance to the extent necessary in order to pay no further premiums. This may represent as little as 5% to 20% decrease in the original face value.

If you are called upon for additional premiums and your spouse is deceased and your own health is questionable, there would be little reason to pay additional money if the policy will outlive you even with increased mortality or lower interest costs.

As used throughout this book, the philosophy of life insurance is that it should be purchased strictly for death benefit. Therefore, there is no interest in providing excess monies to any insurance company in order to produce higher cash values. *Why pay up to 30% more for the same coverage?*

There are, however, some policies which do not provide the ability for you to eliminate as much of the cash value as possible. In this case, Universal Life shines, since it does give you the ability to design a policy with a minimum cash value while at the same time reducing the premium in order to produce maximum insurance at a minimum price. Many companies producing dividend policies try to compete by utilizing term riders and a combination whole life and term "blended" policy that reduces the cash value as well as the premium. But, they do not have the total flexibility that is available with Universal Life. In any event, this should not preclude you from using these type of policies. Just remember, when used to accomplish the concepts described throughout these pages, insurance is an investment tool. *You wouldn't pay more for an equal return on any other investment and you shouldn't do so with your insurance coverage.* Buy the most amount of insurance for the least amount of money. Why would you give an insurance company more than you have to?

THIN vs. FAT POLICY

You can save up to 30% on your insurance cost by purchasing a thin policy vs. a fat policy.

Highest Cash Value – Highest premium

HIGHEST PREMIUM

100% - Whole Life
Universal Life – Full Endowment

15% LOWER PREMIUM

50% Whole Life – 50% Term
Universal Life – 50% Endowment

30% LOWER PREMIUM

Whole Life
Maximum Blend

Universal Life
0 Endowment

If interest goes up - thin policy becomes fat

If interest goes up - fat policy becomes obese

Lowest Cash Value – Lowest Premium

MAXIMUM COVERAGE FOR LOWEST COST

All figures are based on current assumptions. Charts are for illustrative purposes only.

©1994 WEALTH CREATION CENTERS℠ - Barry Kaye Associates

32

Four Ways to Pay Estate Tax

YOU SHOULD HAVE REALIZED by now that there are truly only four ways to pay the estate taxes that will be levied upon your death and will cost your heirs up to 55% of your total worth.

The first way to pay the taxes is by using cash. Your heirs could simply bite the bullet and hand up to 55% of their inheritance over to the government 9 months after your death. Maybe you're worth enough that giving away more than half your estate still leaves what seems like sufficient funds to provide financial security for your heirs. But when you consider that the principal amount they inherit from you will continue to be taxed as it is passed from one generation to the next, it is an unavoidable conclusion that no amount of money is sufficient to endure for long.

Even if you are worth $1 billion, your estate can not survive the ravages of estate taxes for long! Upon your death, your heirs will lose $550 million. Their heirs will lose $248 million leaving $202 million from your original $1 billion. *Three-quarters of your wealth is simply gone within two generations.* (For the sake of this model and the models to come, we are freezing the principal and assuming no growth in successive generations. Of course, there could be additional growth but, as there could also be significant losses due to bad investments, squandering, etc.,—not to mention the loss of value due to inflation—the point is best made and most easily understood on a static basis.) In the next generation, an

161

additional $111 million will be lost to estate taxes leaving only $91 million which will be taxed $50 million leaving $41 million. And so on. When you consider that, at each generation it is likely that your estate will be split by more people, the principal amount they each inherit is even more diminished. And, when you factor in the fact that, in order for the principal to remain intact, each generation must live only off the interest it earns, you can easily see that *no estate can survive multi-generational taxation unprotected.*

Watch what happens if you start with an estate less than $1 billion but still seemingly sufficient to provide security for your heirs. The devastation gets worse faster.

If you're worth $50 million, your heirs will pay $27.5 million in estate taxes leaving $22.5 million. Taxes will take $12 million from your grandchildren leaving them $10 million. Their children will pay $5.5 million and receive only $4.5 million and their children will have only $2.5 million left after they pay $2 million in estate taxes. *Your estate has been effectively decimated after only four generations!*

With a $10 million estate, it takes only three generations before the ravages of estate taxation bring your worth to less than $1 million.

This is, of course, assuming your heirs have the needed cash to pay the dreadful ravages. If they don't, they will have to either borrow the money, paying interest on the loan which will further deplete their resources, or sell property or collectibles at forced liquidation prices, losing up to 50% of the investment's value along the way. *In either case, they will actually inherit even less!*

Using the $50 million estate as a model, if your heirs had to borrow enough to pay the estate taxes due nine months after your death, they would have a loan amount of $27.5 million. With principal and interest payments over the years, the cost of the financed estate taxes would effectively double thereby virtually eliminating the entire estate.

Even greater depletion occurs if they have to sell off parts of the estate at forced liquidation prices to pay the taxes.

If you think your estate is worth $50 million and this is the amount your heirs will inherit but you have not provided estate tax protection, you could be tragically wrong. If required to sell at forced liquidation prices, your heirs may find your property is really only worth $30 million—or even less—in today's market under the desperate circumstances of having to sell to meet the tax costs. Though estate taxes on the newly-devalued estate are "only" $16.5 million, as opposed to the $27.5 million assessed against $50 million, your heirs will have left only $13.5 million as opposed to the $22.5 remaining from the $50 million. An additional $9 million has been lost.

Clearly, only the fourth method of paying the estate taxes—life insurance purchased through an irrevocable trust—provides a safe, viable, financially sensible means of protecting your estate value. Only insurance purchased through an irrevocable trust discounts your estate tax costs by allowing you to "pay as you go."

For a cost of only $2.75 million, a one-pay, last-to-die life insurance policy will pay the entire $27.5 million in estate taxes leaving your heirs the entire $50 million, assuming you and your spouse are average age 60 and based on current assumptions. At age 70, the policy would cost $5.5 million and, at age 80, it would cost $9.1 million. *In all cases, no matter your age, the cost is far, far less than any other alternative available.* Even if you are uninsurable, utilizing the surrogate insured plan or second generation program described earlier will provide the financial protection you need at a fraction of what any other plan would cost your heirs.

4 WAYS YOUR HEIRS CAN PAY ESTATE TAXES OF $5,000,000

Cash

1

Nine months after the death of you and your spouse, your heirs will have to come up with a huge cash payment.

Forced Liquidation

2

If your estate isn't cash rich, your heirs may have to sell off your property, stocks, etc...usually at huge discounts.

Take out a loan

3

With a $5,000,000 loan repaid over 15 years, your heirs will end up paying DOUBLE ($10,000,000 principal and interest).

DIE RICH

4

Make it easy for your heirs. Purchase a life insurance policy for $500,000—All of your estate tax cost will be paid at a 90% discount.

All figures are based on current assumptions. Charts are for illustrative purposes only. This illustration used a last-to-die insurance policy for a male and female both age 60.
©1994 WEALTH CREATION CENTERS℠ - Barry Kaye Associates

33

$20 Million at No Cost

MANY OF THE INSURANCE VEHICLES recommended in this book and utilized in the sample programs are relatively new to the insurance market. As the uses of life insurance for estate tax planning, wealth creation and preservation have increased, the insurance industry has responded by offering new and different types of policies, premium payment options, and coverage options. This is important to know because many people who purchased insurance prior to the changes taking place are now disadvantaged by antiquated policies.

One of the best results of the changes in how life insurance is purchased is that older policies can often be optimized to yield far greater returns.

If you already have insurance and are thinking that it will provide the estate protection you desire, you may be shortchanging your heirs by as much as 300%! In other words, the same cost could provide 3 times as much return.

Many of the older policies which people have do not use a last-to-die approach. Often, a man's life was insured under the assumption that, as the major wage earner and financial partner in a marriage, his loss would be the one to most direly affect the family fortune. While this can well be true when purchasing insurance on younger people as a hedge against a financial tragedy, it is not effective when the insurance purchase is intended to recover estate tax losses for your heirs. Since they will not inherit the estate and have to pay taxes until after the passing of both parents, a last-to-die policy is far more efficient and provides a much greater return.

Many other of the old policies were purchased on a lifetime pay basis. Basically, you financed the purchase by paying premiums every year. Though this had the effect of making the premiums seem less, in fact you paid more, as you do on any financed purchase. By collecting only a portion of the total needed each year, the insurance company has less money on which to earn income and therefore the overall cost goes up. The newer one-pay, five-pay and ten-pay policies significantly shorten the term of payment and are more cash demanding, but the overall cost goes down.

In some cases, existing policies can be optimized to net the greatest return with the least cost under today's assumptions. Sometimes cash values can be taken from an older policy and used to purchase additional new insurance to cover the difference between the amount needed and the amount the current policy will return at no additional cost to you.

In other cases, the policies are so outdated and not cost efficient that the best course of action is to terminate them and start over.

Consider the case of a man who has a $100 million estate and requires $55 million in insurance to discount his estate tax costs 91%. He purchased an insurance policy on himself years ago. For a cost of $190 thousand per year his heirs were to receive $8.7 million upon his death.

By changing his coverage to the newer last-to-die policies, insuring both he and his wife, he will receive a much greater return. The same $190 thousand per year will now purchase $29 million. *His heirs receive $20 million more for the same cost—an increase in return of over 300%—virtually no cost additional insurance.*

Another example would be that of a man who held an antiquated $7.5 million last-to-die insurance policy. Though the policy was properly structured within an irrevocable trust, was appropriately based on him and his wife, and arranged to pay off on the second death in order to offset the estate taxes that would then be due, it included $190 thousand of cash value. Furthermore, due to changes in interest rates from the original assumptions, the projected premium cost of $87 thousand annually had increased from the original seven payments to twenty payments plus.

By transferring the existing cash value to a new policy, based on current assumptions, the man was able to buy a new $7.5 million policy for only $75 thousand a year over a twelve year period. This resulted in a savings of $12 thousand a year for a total of $144 thousand as well as an additional savings of at least $87 thousand for the next five years—a total of approximately $600 thousand. *The final result—the same insurance proceeds of $7.5 million in the same irrevocable trust. However, at a total cost savings of over $600 thousand!*

If the man could afford the original payments, the savings could be re-invested and used to purchase additional death benefits. Then, for the same amount as he was currently spending, the insurance benefit could be increased to $10 million—$2.5 million more for the same money!

$20 MILLION AT NO COST

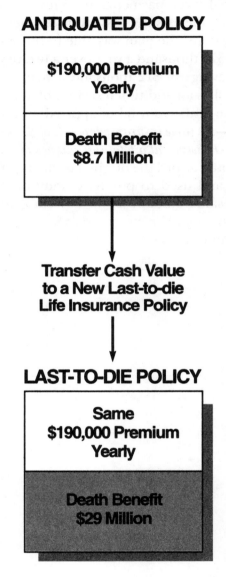

ANTIQUATED POLICY

$190,000 Premium
Yearly

Death Benefit
$8.7 Million

Transfer Cash Value
to a New Last-to-die
Life Insurance Policy

LAST-TO-DIE POLICY

Same
$190,000 Premium
Yearly

Death Benefit
$29 Million

All figures are based on current assumptions. Charts are for illustrative purposes only.

34

Your Ultimate Beneficiary is America

As TAX INCREASE DEBATES ARE WAGED in Congress, a lot of good citizens who have profited by the freedom and opportunity America represents have been heard to say, "I don't mind paying a little bit more if it means the best for my country." As laudable as that sentiment is, it is unnecessary. *Most of the programs outlined in this book do not take one single penny of his due from Uncle Sam. In fact, by preserving wealth through the use of life insurance and an irrevocable trust, the ultimate beneficiary is America.* Not only does the government receive the full estate taxes of up to 55%, but, the amount that is saved makes more investment funds available, generates additional income and generates taxes effectively all paid in perpetuity.

Look at it this way. If you have a $20 million estate, your heirs will pay $11 million in estate taxes upon your death. They will be left with $9 million which, in a world of 5% interest, will earn $450 thousand per year subject to income taxes of about $180 thousand. Over a twenty year span, they will pay $3.6 million in income tax plus the $11 million in initial estate taxes for a total of $14.6 million.

But, if you purchase a life insurance policy to recover the $11 million estate tax loss, your heirs will retain the full $20 million.

The government still gets its $11 million in estate taxes, but, in addition, the $20 million estate now earns $1 million of income on which $400 thousand of income taxes are due per year. Over the same twenty years, that will equal $8 million in income tax over and above the original $11 million for a total of $19 million in government revenues, $4.4 million more.

Everyone wins. The government receives its full estate tax, your heirs receive your full estate and additional income taxes of $220 thousand yearly are generated in perpetuity for Uncle Sam.

But the national benefits do not end there. There is also the increased income earned by the full $20 million estate—$550 thousand more than it would have earned if the $11 million in estate taxes had not been replaced by the insurance—and more than twice the capital exists to fund business and financial opportunities. These increased investments will create more jobs and earn more profits thereby broadening the tax base for the whole country.

For example, suppose your heirs took the $11 million they "saved" and invested it in a business with annual sales of $5 million. If the company earns a 15% profit margin, its taxable income would be $750 thousand, the tax on which would be approximately $250 thousand. Furthermore, given a modest ratio of employees to sales, combined salaries could realistically be assumed to equal about $700 thousand of adjusted gross income, generating an additional $150 thousand in federal income taxes. *The company and its employees would be paying a combined total of $400 thousand per year in corporate and individual taxes. Over twenty years, this would equal $8 million in tax revenues.*

In contrast, if the heirs had not recovered the $11 million in estate tax costs, they might not have had been able to invest in this business venture. The amount of revenues would be eliminated, the amount of taxes paid on those revenues would be eliminated, the number of employees would be eliminated, the amount of income taxes paid on those employees would be eliminated. Everyone loses. The government gets its full $11 million in estate taxes but it gets less in earned income tax on the remaining $9 million, less in taxes on business revenues, and less total income tax because fewer people are employed. The win-win situation has tragically become a lose-lose—and it was completely avoidable.

YOU WIN – AMERICA WINS

CURRENT METHOD   ## DIE RICH METHOD

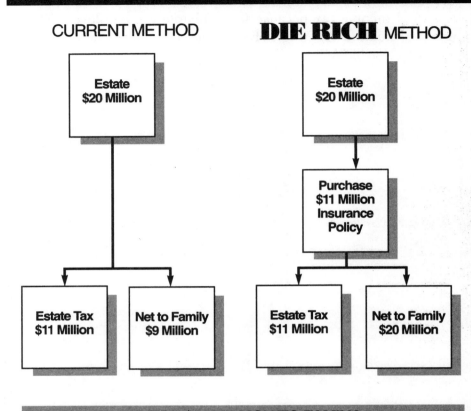

EXTRA $11 MILLION TO FAMILY

EARNS 5% INTEREST — EXTRA $550,000 YEARLY

UNCLE SAM RECEIVES SAME $11 MILLION ESTATE TAX PLUS EXTRA $220,000 INCOME TAX YEARLY IN PERPETUITY

All figures are based on current assumptions. Charts are for illustrative purposes only.

35

Family Partnership

MANY INVESTORS ARE FAMILIAR with the concept of the limited partnership. The limited partnership is a special type of partnership, with all management authority vested in the general partner, who has unlimited liability. The investors in the limited partnership are the limited partners, who generally may not participate in the day-to-day management of the partnership's business. In return for their lack of participation in business operations, the limited partners have only limited liability for partnership debts and obligations, with their liability limited to the amount of investment in the partnership.

Though limited partnerships have been used for many years to own many different types of investments (most notably real estate investments), they have also been used in the intra-family setting to further very important estate planning goals. In this regard, a family limited partnership can provide a very cost effective means of transferring assets to younger family members without giving outright control to those younger family members. Family limited partnerships have also received a great deal of attention in the past few years for two other significant attributes. First, the use of a family limited partnership to hold title to assets may allow the transferors to claim various valuation discounts to reduce the gift and estate tax consequences of the transfer of assets to others. There has been a significant amount of litigation concerning this issue, most of which has to date been resolved in favor of the taxpayer rather than the Internal Revenue Service. Second, the use of a family limited partnership may under certain circumstances provide a measure of protection from creditors.

The typical family limited partnership is established with one or more parents as the general partners. In the alternative, a closely held corporation may act as a general partner. The use of a corporate general partner may result in additional planning opportunities for the family, including the potential availability of corporate fringe benefits and the continuity of existence that only a corporation possesses. Moreover, a corporation which is properly organized and operated may shelter its shareholders from personal liability for corporate actions. Accordingly, even though the general partner of a family limited partnership has unlimited personal liability, if that general partner is a corporation, no individual will be exposed to unlimited personal liability. If the corporate general partner is owned by one or more trusts, then there will not be a need for probate proceedings in the event that the corporation's principals die or become incapacitated.

The limited partners of a family limited partnership may include the parents, the parents' revocable living trust, the children, or one or more types of irrevocable trusts. It is usually advantageous to have the limited partnership interests held by revocable or irrevocable trusts, to obtain the benefits of trust ownership, including probate avoidance. Often the limited partnerships are owned by the parents or their living trusts, with annual gifts being made of limited partnership interests to children, grandchildren or trusts established for their benefit. If those gifts are made over a period of many years, the annual gifts may be small enough to absorb only the $10 thousand per donee annual gift tax exclusion, without using the donor's $600 thousand exemption from estate and gift taxes. In the alternative, the amount of the gifts can be structured to use all or a substantial portion of the $600 thousand exemption. In any event, the transfer of the limited partnership interests does not carry with it a transfer of the management rights of the general partner.

It is important to note that the greatest advantage of the family limited partnership is the fact that transfers of partnership interests may qualify for one or more valuation discounts for estate and gift tax purposes. For example, a partnership may own property with a fair market value of $10 million. A 10% interest in the partnership would be worth $1 million. However, if the partnership is properly structured, the partnership agreement will impose substantial restrictions on the transfer of partnership interests by donees. Accordingly, under recent case law, the donor may claim a minority interest discount and a lack of marketability discount for valuation purposes. Many advisors have suggested that the appropriate range for such discounts may be between 20% and 35%, or more. Accordingly, the value for gift tax purposes of the transferred 10% partnership interest may be between $650 thousand and $800 thousand. The valuation discounts mean that a donor can transfer larger amounts of property for the same gift or estate tax cost.

The same valuation discount concepts apply where a donor has retained a less than 50% interest in the family limited partnership at the time of the donor's death. Under those circumstances, the donor's estate may claim the same minority interest and lack of marketability discounts on the donor's federal estate tax return, which may result in a substantial estate tax savings.

Family limited partnerships may also be structured to "freeze" the value of the donor's interest in partnership assets, to shift future appreciation to the younger generation limited partners. Such partnerships must be structured with great care to avoid problems under the federal estate and gift tax laws concerning valuation of transferred property.

Many promoters have suggested that the family limited partnership can be used to avoid liability to creditors. Some have suggested that persons fearing personal liability should transfer their assets to a family limited partnership. Their analysis is based on the provisions of limited partnership law which limits a creditor's rights to a "charging order" against income distributed to the debtor limited partner. However, the rights of creditors may vary from state to state and creditors may be able to set aside transfers of property to a family limited partnership under certain circumstances (such as a transfer in anticipation of an unfavorable jury verdict against the person establishing the family limited partnership). The laws concerning such transfers are evolving rapidly in many states. Accordingly, you should consult with a local legal counsel before establishing a family limited partnership for this purpose.

36

Home Grit

P.146

An EARLIER CONCEPT rebutted a leading financial newspaper article which recommended the use of a personal residence trust. While, in the instance the article described, a personal residence trust was not the best means of proceeding to accomplish the desired goals, there are times when this sort of trust can be extremely beneficial.

Many estate planning strategies are designed to leverage the donor's $600 thousand exemption from gift and estate taxes. For example, by establishing and funding an irrevocable life insurance trust, a transfer of assets equal to the annual insurance premium for the life insurance held by the trust may result in the beneficiaries of the trust receiving substantially greater benefits (the proceeds of the insurance policy). Similarly, the transfer of limited partnership interests to younger generation family members through annual gifts over a period of years may result in a benefit much greater than the sum of the value of the transferred partnership interests, where the value of the partnership assets increases over time. However, many donors want to retain the benefits from the property which is being transferred to others. These retained interest transfers were historically handled by way of partnership freezes, corporate recapitalizations, and the use of various types of irrevocable trusts.

Many donors used the concept of the Grantor Retained Income

Trust ("GRIT") to transfer property to children and other donees at a reduced gift tax cost. A GRIT is a type of irrevocable trust in which the donor receives the income for a period of years, after which the trust property passes to the children or other donees. The gift to the GRIT must be irrevocable, and the gift to the donees is valued using actuarial tables based on interest rates that change from month to month, as well as on the term of the interest retained by the donor. If the donor dies prior to the expiration of the term, the value of the property held in the GRIT will be included in the donor's estate for federal estate tax purposes. If the donor outlives the term of the GRIT, the trust property will not be included in the donor's estate for federal estate tax purposes. Therefore, if the donor outlives the term of the GRIT, the total transfer tax cost may be a small fraction of the estate tax cost if the GRIT had not been established.

In 1990, Congress changed the tax law provisions concerning GRITs to make them less attractive. Under present law, there are three alternative means of establishing a retained interest trust similar to a GRIT. A donor may establish a Grantor Retained Annuity Trust ("GRAT"), which pays a fixed sum to the donor during the term of the trust, or the donor may create a Grantor Retained Unitrust ("GRUT") which pays a fixed percentage of the fair market value of the trust's assets to the donor, with the assets subject to annual revaluation. The GRAT and GRUT generally provide a smaller estate tax savings than a GRIT, but may be funded with different types of property.

The GRIT is still available, but can now be funded only with a personal residence which constitute's the trust beneficiary's principal or secondary residence. Accordingly, the GRIT is now called a "Qualified Personal Residence Trust" or "QPRT." The IRS has issued lengthy regulations setting forth the operational requirements for a QPRT. In general, the QPRT must hold only a qualified personal residence or the proceeds of sale or condemnation of a qualified personal residence. There are significant limitations on the amount of cash reserves that may be placed in the trust. In addition, the trust must be structured to eliminate the possibility that it will hold nonqualifying assets, such as business interests or rental property.

Even though there may be substantial estate tax advantages to the establishment of a QPRT, there are significant practical disadvantages as well. First, the ultimate beneficiaries of the QPRT will receive the donor's income tax basis in the residence, rather than a step-up or step-down in income tax basis. Accordingly, the ultimate beneficiaries may have to pay a significant capital gains tax in the event that the property is sold. Second, it may be very difficult for an individual to knowingly relinquish the individual's home, since the donor will have no interest in the trust property once the trust term has been completed. Though a QPRT does not have to be structured to give the property outright to the ultimate beneficiaries (for example, it could mirror the dispositive provisions of the donor's revocable living trust), there may be some discomfort in knowing that the donor no longer owns his or her home. In this regard, the parties could agree that the donor would rent the property from the QPRT after the expiration of the donor's retained interest term. The payment of rent would provide yet another means to transfer assets to the ultimate beneficiaries of the QPRT. However, the donor may simply not be comfortable with the concept of losing control of his or her home.

The QPRT is an excellent planning tool for the relatively small number of donors who are willing to use it. For the majority of individuals, the QPRT seems to involve the relinquishment of too much control for the benefits received.

37

Reallocation of Assets

Would you pay $6.9 million to recover only $7 million? You would if the alternative were for your family to receive only $3.5 million.

Consider the case of a man with a $15 million estate. He has clearly stated that he intends to give $8 million to his church at his death and this will reduce his estate to $7 million (there will be no estate taxes on the $8 million since it is going to charity). The $8 million earmarked for the charity produces enough income for him to live in accordance with his current lifestyle.

The remaining $7 million of his $15 million estate will go to his children upon his death and is composed of CD's, Muni's and T-Bills. It produces income in excess of what his lifestyle requires, so he simply allows the interest to compound. At his death, the $7 million will be exposed to approximately $3.5 million of estate taxes thus leaving his children only $3.5 million.

By reallocating his assets, the man can produce $7 million after all taxes for his children as opposed to the $3.5 million now planned.

Based on his age of 82, he can purchase a $7 million life insurance policy on a one-payment basis for $4.6 million, based on current assumptions. In order to transfer that sum out of his estate and into an irrevocable trust, he will pay $2.3 million in gift taxes for a total cost of $6.9 million. While this may seem like an outlandish amount of money to pay for an asset that is ultimately worth only $7 million, only $100 thousand more than its cost, the $7 million will come to his family income and estate tax free. *Isn't it better for his children to receive $7 million instead of $3.5 million, no matter how he gets there?*

Truly, in this situation, the end justifies the means. Or, more specifically, the total after tax asset of $7 million to the children justifies the expense of paying $6.9 million to accomplish that end. This is a true example of reallocating your assets in such a manner to optimize money.

The man's income is provided by the $8 million which he has left and which will be gifted to the charity at his death. His children pay no estate taxes on that $8 million and receive an additional $7 million from the insurance proceeds. Though at his age of 82 it cost him $6.9 million to accomplish it, his entire $15 million estate passes on to his charity and family totally intact!

WHEN WOULD YOU PAY $6.9 MILLION FOR $7 MILLION?

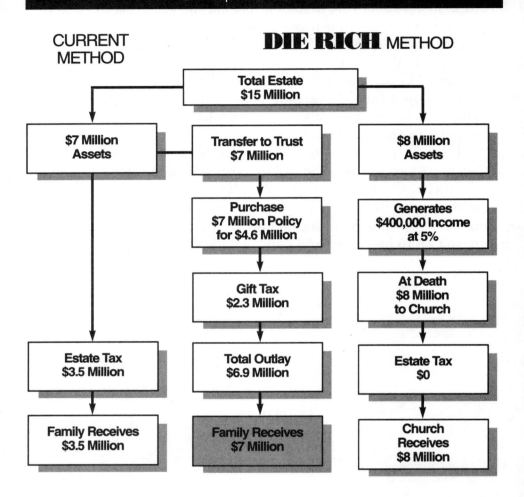

CURRENT METHOD

DIE RICH METHOD

Total Estate
$15 Million

$7 Million
Assets

Transfer to Trust
$7 Million

$8 Million
Assets

Purchase
$7 Million Policy
for $4.6 Million

Generates
$400,000 Income
at 5%

Gift Tax
$2.3 Million

At Death
$8 Million
to Church

Estate Tax
$3.5 Million

Total Outlay
$6.9 Million

Estate Tax
$0

Family Receives
$3.5 Million

Family Receives
$7 Million

Church
Receives
$8 Million

ONLY WHEN IT PRODUCES AN EXTRA $3.5 MILLION

All figures are based on current assumptions. Charts are for illustrative purposes only.
This illustration used an insurance policy for a male age 82.
©1994 WEALTH CREATION CENTERS℠ - Barry Kaye Associates

38

Capital Optimizer—$45 Million
Versus $133 Million

WHEN DO YOU HAVE ENOUGH MONEY? The truest answer is: never! Particularly when you consider that, no matter how large your estate may be, your heirs will only inherit 45% of its value after estate taxes are paid to the government.

This being the case, it only makes sense to do your utmost to optimize your capital and preserve your wealth. The following concept demonstrates a particularly outstanding means for accomplishing this.

Assume you have $100 million (you may make this number larger or smaller by adding or subtracting zeros). At death, $55 million of your $100 million of assets will go out the window in estate taxes. Your children will still inherit $45 million, but if you are willing and able to spend $18 million (based on average age 70) without upsetting your current lifestyle, you will be able to produce $100 million of insurance, based on current assumptions.

You transfer $18 million to an irrevocable trust. You will then pay approximately $10 million in gift taxes. Of course, if you wait until death for your money to transfer from your estate, there will be no gift taxes to pay. However, there will be the $55 million in estate taxes which can be avoided by paying the $10 million in gift taxes now. Obviously, it makes a lot more sense to pay the smaller gift tax on the $18 million gift than the $55 million estate tax on the $100 million policy.

More importantly, in paying the gift taxes of $10 million*, you will remove from your estate both the $18 million which paid the insurance premium as well as the $10 million to pay the gift taxes. This results in your having $28 million less of assets to be taxed, thus producing a savings of approximately $16 million in estate taxes. Your $100 million estate would have been taxed $55 million leaving your heirs $45 million. Now your $72 million estate will only be taxed $39.6 million leaving $32.4 million. So, in effect, the real cost of the program is only $12.6 million.

The $18 million in the irrevocable trust purchases a $100 million policy. *Added to the $32.4 million which remains after taxes are paid on the $72 million balance of your estate, this means your children will inherit $132.4 million—net after all gift and estate taxes! That's almost three times the $45 million they would have received otherwise.*

This is truly a method of optimizing your capital. Since you must die, why not produce the maximum amount of money at the time of your death, which is the time that all of your assets go to your heirs.

$133 million or $45 million. It's a large difference—and the choice is completely up to you!

---

* Gift tax paid within three years of the death of the donor will be includable in the gross estate.

REALLOCATE YOUR ASSETS & OPTIMIZE YOUR CAPITAL

	CURRENT METHOD	DIE RICH METHOD
Estate Value	$100,000,000	$100,000,000
Buy $100 Million One-pay Insurance Policy	$0	($18,000,000)
Gift Tax	$0	($10,000,000)
Assets at Death	$100,000,000	$72,000,000
Estate Tax	($55,000,000)	($39,000,000)
Net Assets	$45,000,000	$33,000,000
Insurance Pays	$0	$100,000,000
Net to Family	$45,000,000	$133,000,000

INCREASE WHAT YOU LEAVE TO YOUR FAMILY 3 TIMES

All figures are based on current assumptions. Charts are for illustrative purposes only.
This illustration used a last-to-die insurance policy for a male and female both age 70.
©1994 WEALTH CREATION CENTERS℠ - Barry Kaye Associates

THE MOST OVERLOOKED INVESTMENT STRATEGY

For those worth $100 Million or More —

Buy a $100 Million Last-to-die Life Insurance Policy

Each Policy Matures at the Death of the Second Spouse, Income and Estate Tax Free!

If you have principal that you don't wish to risk or excess income beyond what your lifestyle requires, this is the best investment strategy for you!

Age	1 Payment To Ins. Co.	Gift Tax To Uncle Sam	Total Outlay		DIE RICH Method	Current Method	Why Lose?
60	$10 Million	$5 Million	$15 Million	Buys	$100 Million	$7 Million	$93 Million
65	$13 Million	$7 Million	$20 Million	Buys	$100 Million	$9 Million	$91 Million
70	$18 Million	$10 Million	$28 Million	Buys	$100 Million	$13 Million	$87 Million
75	$23 Million	$13 Million	$36 Million	Buys	$100 Million	$16 Million	$84 Million
80	$35 Million	$19 Million	$54 Million	Buys	$100 Million	$25 Million	$75 Million

Also available in smaller amounts. Add or remove a zero for larger or smaller estates.

The only cost to you is the yearly loss of interest on your total outlay!

Age 60	$750,000
Age 65	$1,007,500
Age 70	$1,395,000
Age 75	$1,782,000
Age 80	$2,712,500

WHERE CAN YOU INVEST $750,000 - $2,712,500 YEARLY & RECEIVE $100 MILLION?

All figures are based on current assumptions. Charts are for illustrative purposes only.
This plan can be financed over a period of time.
©1994 WEALTH CREATION CENTERS℠ - Barry Kaye Associates

39

A Different Perspective— $400 Thousand Debt Repayment Becomes $2 Million Liquid Funds

As CHANGES IN THE INSURANCE INDUSTRY are effected and uses for insurance are expanded, many people fail to grasp some of the newest concepts and, as a result, lose out on opportunities to optimize their financial situations. Accountants, attorneys and laypeople can all get stuck in old ways of thinking that are no longer the most effective or pertinent means of planning.

For many years, the common wisdom was to live as debt free as possible. People with the means to do so paid off all debt in the mistaken belief that to do so was the best means of ensuring their financial stability. But often the money used to pay off existing debt can be better utilized in such a way that the debt payment is optimized many times over.

Consider the case of man who has $5 million is assets composed of $600 thousand in municipal bonds, $100 thousand in regular bonds and approximately $3.5 million in real estate. He has no debt against the real estate except for $400 thousand which is currently costing approximately $24 thousand a year. The man's income is $200 thousand per year and the $24 thousand in interest payments are already part of his budget; it will not negatively impact his lifestyle in any way to continue making these $24 thousand yearly payments.

The man thinks he should pay off the $400 thousand debt and be done with it, then his property will be totally unencumbered. But, if he pays off the $400 thousand, he will be exchanging $400 thousand of liquid cash for $400 thousand of a loan note. It is an even exchange dollar for dollar—$400 thousand of cash flow for $400 thousand removal of debt.

If, instead, the man were to take the $400 thousand and purchase a life insurance policy, his heirs could receive a 5–1 return of $2 million—or more, depending on his age and current assumptions.

Upon his death, the $400 thousand of added equity to his real estate accomplished by paying off the outstanding debt will be subject to estate tax of 50%. His heirs will really only realize $200 thousand benefit from the loan repayment. But the $2 million insurance proceeds, purchased through an irrevocable trust, will come to his heirs income and estate tax free; they will retain their full value. If a forced liquidation is necessary to pay the estate taxes, the $400 thousand may result in only $300 thousand thus producing as little as $150 thousand after estate taxes. In addition, there is an added tax benefit in that the man's estate will have been reduced by the $400 thousand insurance premium payment and so his heirs will "save" an additional $200 thousand in estate taxes.

By paying off the debt, the man would effectively pass only $150 to $200 thousand more on to his heirs. By allowing the debt to continue, he provides them with $1.6 million ($2 million less $400 thousand) at a cost of only $24 thousand per year. It would seem that a new perspective could pay off.

$400,000 DEBT FUNDS BECOME $2 MILLION

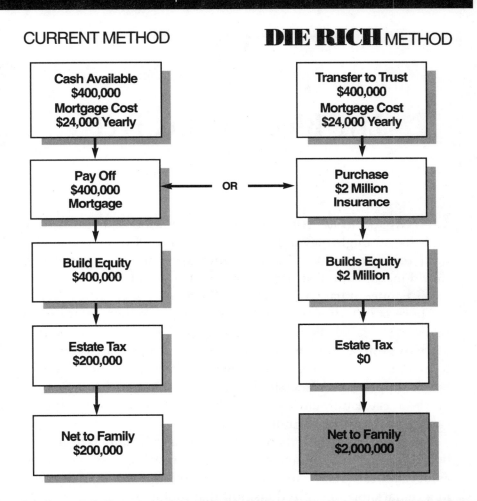

CURRENT METHOD

Cash Available
$400,000
Mortgage Cost
$24,000 Yearly

↓

Pay Off
$400,000
Mortgage

↓

Build Equity
$400,000

↓

Estate Tax
$200,000

↓

Net to Family
$200,000

DIE RICH METHOD

Transfer to Trust
$400,000
Mortgage Cost
$24,000 Yearly

↓

Purchase
$2 Million
Insurance

↓

Builds Equity
$2 Million

↓

Estate Tax
$0

↓

Net to Family
$2,000,000

← OR →

FOR $24,000 YEARLY, FAMILY RECEIVES EXTRA $1.8 MILLION

All figures are based on current assumptions. Charts are for illustrative purposes only.
This illustration used a last-to-die insurance policy for a male and female both age 70.
©1994 WEALTH CREATION CENTERS℠ - Barry Kaye Associates

40

Live Rich and Tax Free

Upon hearing of the advent of this new book, many people said that, though they did want to die rich and though they did want to leave their children financially secure and protected, they'd just as soon live rich as long as they could.

This concept has been included for them.

There is one drawback to the following program, however. It really isn't viable for anyone under age 75. In fact, its benefit increases with age and as health deteriorates. There are other ways to increase the potential for living rich, some were included earlier on in previous discussions of immediate annuities. This one, however, is the ultimate expression of maximizing and leveraging capital during your lifetime. At least . . . it is for now.

Using the plan described below, you can virtually pull money out of thin air to enhance your current lifestyle. In addition, the asset reallocation effected will provide you with this extra income in a remarkably optimized fashion that includes:

- No Capital Gains Tax
- No Income Tax
- No Estate Tax
- No Gift Tax
- No Alternative Minimum Tax
- No Loss of Current Income

· No Loss of Future Appreciation of Gross Stock Portfolio
· No Cash Flow Impairment Whatsoever

How is all this possible? Here's how:

For the sake of this example, assume a man and his wife, together averaging age 80, have a $15 million stock portfolio. (To customize the example to your own situation, add or subtract a zero as appropriate.)

The couple takes advantage of the margin available through their stock brokerage firm and borrow $1.5 million against their holdings. In so doing, they have not paid any capital gains tax or diminished their stock portfolio in any way—it continues earning the same returns and maintains its future appreciation ability.

Using the $1.5 million, they purchase an immediate annuity on themselves which will produce a guaranteed annual income for as long as one of them is alive. In so doing, *they will guarantee a capital transfer of $1.5 million to their son, income and estate tax free, create additional annual income for themselves and reduce their estate by $1.5 million which reduces the estate tax liability by $750 thousand.* All this at no cost to themselves whatsoever.

At their ages, and based on current assumptions, the immediate annuity which they purchased with the borrowed $1.5 million produces annual income of $191 thousand after taxes for their life expectancy. From that, they pay the $75 thousand annual interest due on the loan. This leaves $116 thousand. From that, they pay $71 thousand annually in premium payments on a $1.5 million last-to-die policy placed within an irrevocable trust for the ultimate benefit of their son. As a result, upon the last death, he will receive $1.5 million, income and estate tax free, which will replace the $1.5 million principal of the loan from the stock brokerage firm. This transfer of capital occurs in such a manner that no gift taxes are due on it and the proceeds come to their son free from estate or income tax liability.

The loan interest payments are made each year with proceeds from the annuity and the principal is recovered by the insurance which is also paid for in full by the annuity income. And, in addition, there is $45 thousand *a year in extra income for the couple, virtually pulled out of thin air!* Furthermore, their son will also benefit from a $750 thousand estate tax reduction which represents the taxes avoided by the transfer of $1.5 million out of their estate.

An extra $45 thousand a year, for each and every year that one of the couple is alive, has been created with no tax liability and no loss of previous income or investment potential. Truly this concept has accomplished its goal of creating new means for people to *Live* Rich and Tax Free!

As an aside—should the couple decide they don't actually need the extra $45 thousand in annual income, they could use it towards the purchase, even at their ages, of an additional $1 million in life insurance for their son. The total cost of a $1 million last-to-die policy on them, based on current assumptions, would be $50 thousand. So, for $5 thousand a year, effectively, they could transfer $1.5 million out of their estate and their son would realize $750 thousand in estate tax savings plus an additional $1 million in insurance proceeds—all of it income and estate tax free. *He would receive a total of $2.25 million at an effective cost of only $5 thousand per year!* If he qualified, all estate taxes could be paid at no cost to him whatsoever. This is the optimum of "Live Rich and Tax Free."

LIVE RICH!

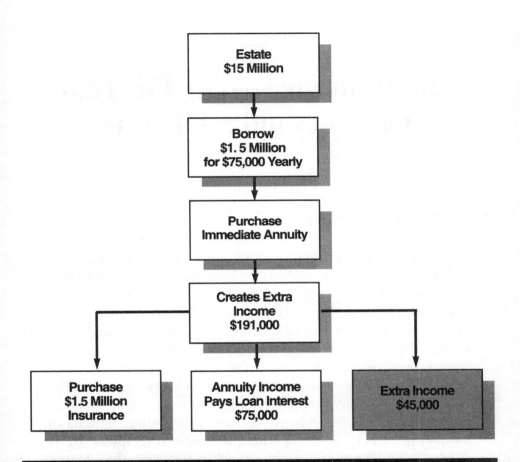

```
            ┌─────────────────┐
            │     Estate      │
            │   $15 Million   │
            └────────┬────────┘
                     │
                     ▼
            ┌─────────────────┐
            │     Borrow      │
            │   $1. 5 Million  │
            │ for $75,000 Yearly │
            └────────┬────────┘
                     │
                     ▼
            ┌─────────────────┐
            │    Purchase     │
            │ Immediate Annuity │
            └────────┬────────┘
                     │
                     ▼
            ┌─────────────────┐
            │  Creates Extra  │
            │     Income      │
            │    $191,000     │
            └─────────────────┘
```

| Purchase $1.5 Million Insurance | Annuity Income Pays Loan Interest $75,000 | Extra Income $45,000 |

PULL $45,000 OUT OF THIN AIR!

All figures are based on current assumptions, current taxes and life expectancy. Charts are for illustrative purposes only. This illustration used a last-to-die insurance policy for a male and female both age 85.

©1994 WEALTH CREATION CENTERS℠ - Barry Kaye Associates

41

Life Insurance—The Gift That Lasts Beyond a Lifetime

❦ The Ultimate Gift

What is a legacy? An inheritance passed from one generation to the next. In reality, it is nothing more than a gift. A loving gift of the assets you have produced in your lifetime for the benefit of your posterity. It is truly a lasting and very special present, the gifting of all or some part of yourself, in the form of your possessions and property, to someone you love. The gift of enhanced financial security to ease the way for the next generation. These gifts transcend any discussion of assets, taxes or legal ramifications. They defy any financial measurement or value. They are measured more accurately in the feelings of safety, satisfaction and pleasure they confer on both gift giver and recipient. In the sense of fulfillment you enjoy knowing that your loved ones' dreams will be consummated as a result of your creativity, ingenuity, vision and knowledge in optimizing and maximizing what they receive after you are gone.

All of the concepts discussed in this book for accomplishing the greatest legacy of financial security are based on a new way of thinking about life insurance. They utilize its incredible leverage to create the ultimate gift of financial security for your loved ones.

What else would you call a method for leaving relatively large sums of money to those nearest to you, or to your favorite charity or cause, at a huge discount if not a truly loving gift that lasts beyond a lifetime?

Imagine taking $142 thousand and turning it into a $1 million gift for someone you love. That would represent an 86% discount on a $1 million gift, based upon current assumptions, at your death. Imagine it as walking into your favorite department store and being able to purchase a $1 million gift certificate for a cost of only 14 cents on the dollar. *An* 86% off sale!

This is what the gift of life insurance can do for you and those you love. It allows you to present them with highly optimized financial gifts, at a fraction of the cost of their ultimate value. These gifts, can be purchased on a one-pay basis or financed on a five-pay, ten-pay or even lifetime payment basis. Let your dreams for those you love be fully realized in the future based on your love and wisdom. Gifts of life insurance can be given in such a manner that the recipient can fully enjoy every possible option during their lifetime or the gift can be tailor-made in accordance with what you believe will be best for them.

The life insurance purchase you make on behalf of your loved ones is nothing less than the ultimate gift which lasts beyond a lifetime by accomplishing tremendous returns at your death for the benefit of your family or other selected heir. These gifts can be structured in such a way as to optimize the return they produce while minimizing the tax aspect of the principal received. In many cases, their purchase has been made so simple and clear as to avoid almost all necessity for legal or financial consultation and it is even possible that, depending on your age and health and the amount you buy, no medical exam will be required.

If you and your wife utilize a last-to-die life insurance policy at an average age 60, one payment of $150 thousand will produce up to $1.5 million for your heirs following the last survivor's death, based on current assumptions. At average age 70, the return is approximately 5 to 1 making the same $150 thousand produce a gift certificate of $750 thousand. Utilizing a last-to-die policy on a couple who are average age 80, the same $150 thousand would purchase $450 thousand realizing a 3 times increase. And, since it is possible to arrange that the proceeds from these gifted policies come to your heirs on a tax free basis, there will be no income or estate tax loss.

The point is, if you are already giving large amounts of money to your children, grandchildren or charity, or if you have been saving whatever you could for their ultimate benefit, you can now use those funds at a great discount and increase their gift many times over.

Think of all the wedding, anniversary, birthday, bar mitzvah, confirmation, and graduation gifts you make. Do you give cash, mutual funds, bonds, store certificates? The gift is no doubt greatly appreciated. But what if the gift could be as much as ten times greater without it costing you anything more? Wouldn't that be even better and more appreciated. Using life insurance as a method to create the ultimate gift, that is exactly what transpires.

This really has nothing to do with insurance. Insurance is simply the vehicle which is used to provide, based on current assumptions, the maximum optimization of your gift. Many people will use these methods to create wealth for their heirs and loved ones. Others will use them to preserve the wealth they have already achieved from the ravages of estate taxation. In either case, the insurance purchase becomes the ultimate expression of your love.

This is not a legal or accounting decision. Only you can determine whether you wish to create this type of gift. There is only one situation in which you absolutely *should not* give these gifts, no matter how much you want to benefit your children.

If you need the principal which you are considering using for the purchase of a gift policy to support your own lifestyle, *this program should not be undertaken.* If transferring this money diminishes income you need to preserve your way of life, this program is not for you. Only money that is surplus, excess or discretionary, money that comes from "the bottom of your pile" or has been saved and specially earmarked for your children's benefit, should be invested in these gift concepts. *The well-being of you and your spouse must come first before that of any child, grandchild, relative or charity.* After all, you will be dead a lot longer than you will have been alive and you must savor each moment of your own life first. Only after you have taken care of yourself can this outstanding, exciting new approach be fully and unequivocally endorsed.

Read the following letters. They are samples of some of the sentiments and occasions which have prompted people to make the ultimate gift of a life insurance policy. See if you would like to share these emotions with people close to you. And, if so, feel free to use these samples to express your own feelings when you present your loved ones with the gift that lasts beyond a lifetime.

❧ *Simply because we love you:*

Through the years we have watched with wonder as you have grown and matured into the most beautiful person of our dreams.

You have enriched our lives each and every day. We have learned so much from who you are and what you are, and we are proud of all that you have achieved in your life.

You are our very special gift.

It is our hope that the beauty of this lasting gift will truly express our everlasting love for you. And, we want the financial security that this gift represents to allow you to enjoy life to its fullest, as we have enjoyed our life with you.

You deserve the best.

With all our love,

❧ *From a grandparent at the birth of his/her grandchild:*

You are a miracle. A gift of life brought to this world by two lives we treasure.

We look forward to the years before you with great anticipation and hope that all your dreams will come true.

On this momentous occasion of your birth, we want to give you a precious, lasting gift that represents a secure and meaningful future for you. A future that allows you to enjoy life to its fullest and never lets your dreams pass you by.

Love life as we love you and seize every opportunity that the miracle of birth presents.

We wish you a lifetime of love and happiness.

❦ *From parents or grandparents at the wedding of their children or grandchildren:*

As you look forward to your new lives together, we share in your love and in your joy. Cherish every moment you spend together as we have cherished every moment we have spent with you.

We want each day of your lives to be filled with as much love and happiness as you have brought to us.

It is our hope that this loving gift will be as lasting and meaningful as your marriage, and will provide you with the financial security to make all your dreams a reality.

May the union of your spirits be blessed with unwavering love, understanding and prosperity.

❧ *To a special advisor or associate:*

You have stood by my side for so many years, supporting me with the loving care of a dear friend and the thoughtful guidance of a wise advisor.

Together we have created something that could never be accomplished alone. You have helped me to achieve what I never thought possible and you have kept me on a narrow path with your wisdom, your strength and your unwavering devotion.

I want to take care of you and your family, as you have taken care of me and mine for so long. It is my hope that this lasting gift will express my profound appreciation for all you have given me and that it will give you the opportunity to enjoy your life to the fullest.

My deepest gratitude to you always.

❧ *To a special friend:*

The greatest gift of all is friendship.

I feel so blessed to have you as a friend. You have given me your heart and shared your soul. You have shown me things about myself only a true friend can reveal. And, you have always been there for me when I needed a shoulder to lean on, a good laugh or a helping hand.

I cherish the memories of our time together and I want our friendship to live on forever, from our hearts to the hearts of our families.

This lasting gift is the legacy of friendship I want to leave for you and for your family, so they will always remember that the loving bonds of friendship can never be severed.

Forever your friend,

❧ *On a special occasion:*

On this momentous occasion, I want to give you a truly lasting and valuable gift that expresses the depth of my affection for you.

You have given so much to me and everyone around you throughout your precious life. I now want to honor you with a special gift that is a part of me.

It is my hope that the financial security this gift represents will give you the opportunity to live the life you have always dreamed about.

You deserve the very best.

Part Two

❦

PROSPECT AND CLIENT EXAMPLES

On the previous pages, samples of the incredible leverage of life insurance, used in conjunction with irrevocable trusts, charitable remainder trusts, grantor-retained income trusts and generation skipping trusts, demonstrated a creative variety of means to create and preserve wealth.

Using the principles described, programs can be customized to accommodate any estate value, marital status, age and financial goal. The benefits of life insurance, purchased through a trust so it is received income and estate tax free, coupled with its guaranteed investment return, are already being used by some of America's wealthiest families to avoid the multi-generational ravages of estate taxation.

Following are 12 actual stories from clients and prospects who have been shown how to realize huge savings using these methods. Obviously, their names have been deleted to protect their financial privacy. But each example is a true recounting of the means employed to secure financial security for their heirs.

You will see from these examples the difference accomplished by using these programs . . . you will see the vast problem-solving potentials of the methods described in Part One . . . you will see how more and more of America's wealthiest families, with access to our nation's top advisors and planners, ultimately realize that no other financial vehicle can equal the power of life insurance in ensuring their children's security.

1

Free Home and
$1.95 Million Profit

I SOLD AN APARTMENT I owned in New York City to an older couple for approximately $1.75 million in 1985. The annual maintenance cost for the residence, including property taxes and maid service, was about $50 thousand per year.

After the sale was consummated, the buyers told me they were familiar with my concepts and wondered what I could do to help protect their estate for their children.

I asked them if they might be interested in recovering for their family the entire $1.75 million cost they paid, effectively making the apartment free and, at the same time, paying, on a tax free basis, their yearly maintenance costs. They said, "Well, of course we would," and asked me to proceed with the arrangements.

I instructed the couple to transfer $1 million to a life insurance company. This purchased a $3.5 million policy on the wife as the man was uninsurable. By their having done so, upon her death, their children would receive back the $1.75 million purchase price for the apartment as well as the $1 million policy cost. The balance of approximately $750 thousand would remain in the policy and would be available, over a period of time, to absorb tax free loans of $50 thousand which they would take to pay the apartment maintenance costs.

In this way, we had delivered a return of the full insurance premium, recovered the full cash price of the property and made available the money for the maintenance on a tax free, cash-flow no-impairment basis.

About five years later, the couple revealed that they had never taken the $50 thousand maintenance loans which we had structured into the arrangement. Therefore, the policy had accrued more cash value than was necessary. Upon analysis, I found that they could purchase a new $4.7 million policy by simply making a 1035 tax free exchange of the cash value from the existing $3.5 million policy to a new $4.7 million policy, with no additional cost or premiums, based on the then-current assumptions. This maximized their death benefit which, by this time, was their primary goal in order to help their children accommodate some of the anticipated estate taxes. With the new $4.7 million policy, the children will receive back the full $1.750 million cost of the apartment, the cost of the insurance, which remained $1 million, and an additional $1.95 million.

RECOVER COST OF $1,750,000 HOME

Purchase Real Estate for $1.75 Million

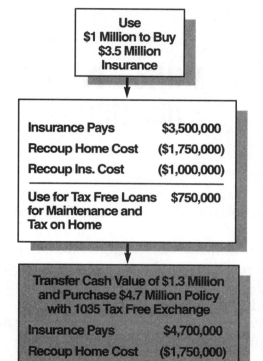

**Use
$1 Million to Buy
$3.5 Million
Insurance**

Insurance Pays	$3,500,000
Recoup Home Cost	($1,750,000)
Recoup Ins. Cost	($1,000,000)
Use for Tax Free Loans for Maintenance and Tax on Home	$750,000

**Transfer Cash Value of $1.3 Million
and Purchase $4.7 Million Policy
with 1035 Tax Free Exchange**

Insurance Pays	$4,700,000
Recoup Home Cost	($1,750,000)
Recoup Insurance	($1,000,000)
Net to Family	$1,950,000

ENJOY FREE HOME + EXTRA $1.95 MILLION

All figures are based on current assumptions. Charts are for illustrative purposes only.
This illustration used an insurance policy for a female age 72.
©1994 WEALTH CREATION CENTERS℠ - Barry Kaye Associates

2

$5 Million Protects
$100 Million

I WAS APPROACHED by the representative of a brokerage firm on behalf of one of his clients. The client was a man in Texas, the founder of a company there, whose business was involved in a leveraged buyout that would gross him $100 million. As this buyout represented significant wealth creation for the man, the brokerage firm had come to us to see if any of our wealth preservation techniques could be utilized for the benefit of the man's family; he wanted to pass on as much of the $100 million estate intact as possible.

"Your client," I explained to the brokerage firm representative, "has two options. He can take the full $100 million, in which case he will suffer considerable capital gains taxes of about $28 million leaving $72 million to his heirs on which they will pay $39 million in estate taxes with a resultant total inheritance of only about $33 million. Or, if that is unacceptable, we can structure an arrangement whereby your client only gets $95 million but provides for a complete recovery by his heirs of the full $28 million income tax and eventual $39 million of estate taxes. Which do you think he would prefer?"

Obviously, the brokerage firm representative replied that his client would prefer the $95 million full recovery plan.

I instructed the representative to have his client transfer the $5 million difference between the $100 million and the $95 million to an irrevocable trust. Based on the current assumptions, the man's age, health, marital status, etc., that $5 million would purchase a life insurance policy worth $69 million. Though there would be some gift tax required for the transfer, it would be minimal, even negligible, in proportion to the wealth preservation which would be accomplished.

At the time of the man's death, the $69 million in insurance policy proceeds would recover for his heirs virtually all of the income and estate tax costs which the buy out had produced. The cost for this benefit was less than the income tax increase would have been if he sold out 5 years later!

$5 MILLION PROTECTS $100 MILLION

	CURRENT METHOD	DIE RICH METHOD
Leveraged Buyout	$100,000,000	$95,000,000
Buy $67 Million of Insurance	$0	($5,000,000)
Capital Gains Tax	($28,000,000)	($28,000,000)
Net Assets	$72,000,000	$67,000,000
Estate Tax	($37,000,000)	($36,000,000)
Insurance Pays	$0	$67,000,000
Net to Family	$33,000,000	$97,000,000

$95 MILLION DIE-RICH METHOD VIRTUALLY TRIPLES NET ESTATE

All figures are based on current assumptions. Charts are for illustrative purposes only.
This illustration used a last-to-die insurance policy for a male and female both age 55.
©1994 WEALTH CREATION CENTERS℠ - Barry Kaye Associates

3

Maximizing a Lottery in Perpetuity

"I've just won the lottery!" an excited voice exclaimed from the other end of the phone, "$4 million!"

"But now I've got a problem," the man went on to say after I'd offered my congratulations.

He'd discovered what many people in similar situations realize after the initial rejoicing has died down—that sudden increases in wealth, especially those which will be paid out over time such as his lottery winnings, sweepstakes prizes, royalties, etc., carry a double-edged sword of estate tax difficulties. After being informed of the liabilities of his situation, the man, a pilot by trade, had read my book, *Save A Fortune On Your Estate Taxes*, and was now calling for help.

The pilot's $4 million winnings were to be paid out at the rate of $140 thousand per year for 28 years. Perhaps, if he lived the full 28 years, he might wind up spending the bulk of that income and reduce it so that estate taxes wouldn't be a tremendous problem. But, if he were to die before the term was up, the government, invoking a tax section known as "Income In Respect Of A Decedant," would levy estate taxes based on the current value of the promised income for the next twenty years. In other words, the government figures out what the present value of the promised lottery payments are today, and uses that figure in assessing the estate taxes. That figure is then added to the already existing estate the man may have for a combined total estate tax liability. Given that the pilot had other assets, if he were to die the next day, his family could be charged estate taxes on a total of $4 million even though he had not collected those dollars as yet from the lottery winnings.

Needless to say, the pilot was very concerned and upset. Where would his family get the money to pay the taxes? They would probably have to borrow against the lottery income devaluating it considerably. Suddenly his great fortune could become a tax nightmare for his loved ones.

I reassured him that his problem was a surmountable one.

The estate taxes on his total $4 million estate (including his existing assets plus the projected value of his $4 million lottery prize) would be about $2 million. The cost of a last-to-die life insurance policy purchased to cover that $2 million would be $15 thousand a year for 15 years, based on his and his wife's average age and the current assumptions of interest and mortality. The policy would pay off the $2 million at the time of the second death, the same time the estate taxes would be due. With $140 thousand per year in guaranteed income from the lottery, money which he would not have had otherwise, he could surely afford the $15 thousand annual premium and his children would be protected even if he died the next day.

"But what if I don't die?" the pilot then questioned. "It's likely that my wife and I will use some, if not all, of that income to live on, particularly after I retire. So there won't be as much left to be taxed."

In that case, I explained, your children will still receive $2 million after your deaths, on which they won't need to pay estate taxes. You won't have lost anything, since the $15 thousand per year premium cost was purely extra income anyway, and they will be financially secure for life.

If they don't need the $2 million to pay the government, those insurance proceeds can remain in the trust where they will produce the same $140 thousand in interest income (assuming a 7% average return over time) as yearly lottery payments. In effect, your children will keep receiving the lottery income forever, and all for a total cost of $225 thousand—$15 thousand a year for 15 years—which is less than 6% of your total lottery winnings.

Without buying a single additional ticket, without having to be chosen from millions of people, the pilot's family could keep winning the lottery again, and again, and again.

WIN THE LOTTERY TWICE

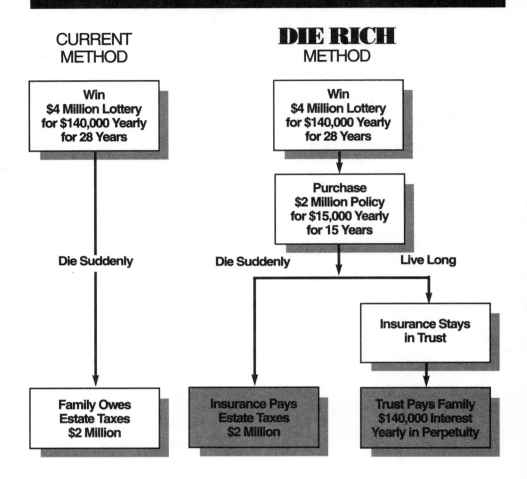

CURRENT METHOD

DIE RICH METHOD

Win $4 Million Lottery for $140,000 Yearly for 28 Years

Win $4 Million Lottery for $140,000 Yearly for 28 Years

Purchase $2 Million Policy for $15,000 Yearly for 15 Years

Die Suddenly

Die Suddenly

Live Long

Insurance Stays in Trust

Family Owes Estate Taxes $2 Million

Insurance Pays Estate Taxes $2 Million

Trust Pays Family $140,000 Interest Yearly in Perpetuity

YOUR FAMILY WINS $140,000 YEARLY IN PERPETUITY

All figures are based on current assumptions. Charts are for illustrative purposes only.
This illustration used a last-to-die insurance policy for a male and female both age 55.
©1994 WEALTH CREATION CENTERS℠ - Barry Kaye Associates

4

Insurance for the Uninsurable

An older man came to me for help in procuring insurance so his children could recover the estate tax loss they would face after his death. Sadly, the man was a widower and too old and ill to be a viable insurance candidate. He had an estate worth about $20 million and wanted very badly to replace the $10 million in estate taxes his children would lose.

"Isn't there anything we can do?" he asked.

I'd been working on a new concept at the time, a plan for surrogate insurance, and the man presented a good opportunity to make it work.

Generally, insurance companies limit policies to direct family lineages (i.e parent to child or grandparent to grandchild). Well, in his speeches, President Clinton often refers to the need for Americans to think of themselves and conduct themselves as if we were all "one big family". I called an insurance company on behalf of this man and explained that if we were all indeed to consider ourselves one big family, surely an aunt or uncle could be reasonably expected to have an interest in the financial welfare of their nieces and nephews.

It took a little doing but eventually the insurance company accepted the logic. They would allow the man's brother and his wife to purchase insurance on behalf of their nephew and niece.

The aunt and uncle were average age 60 and insurable. To

produce $10 million, the insurance would cost $1 million. The man transferred $1 million to an irrevocable trust and then had his brother and his brother's wife examined for the $10 million insurance policy. Upon the brother's and his brother's wife's death (the man's children's uncle and aunt) the policy will produce for the irrevocable trust $10 million. If they die prior to the death of the man, there will be no estate taxes due (this policy is not in their estate) and the money will remain in the irrevocable trust until the father's death. It will then be available to pay the estate taxes due upon his death.

If the man dies first, then the taxes will have to be paid from the estate but will be recovered by the children at the time of their uncle's and aunt death when the life insurance proceeds will replace within the irrevocable trust the taxes that have already been paid.

This is a surrogate insured program. It does the same job as if the man and his wife had been eligible for insurance coverage. Since he was not, the next best thing had been accomplished.

If we'd been unable to utilize a surrogate insured, I had also informed the man that a second alternative existed. Although, without a surrogate insured, the estate taxes would be lost to his children, it would be possible to recover them and even increase the return significantly, for his grandchildren.

The plan would work essentially the same as it would when using the man's brother, only, in this instance, he would use the premium money to purchase a policy on his son for the ultimate benefit of his grandchildren. Given the average ages of his son and his son's wife of 40, a 50–1 return would be realized and $1 million could purchase $40 million. Since this is far in excess of the amount of money required for the situation, $250 thousand could now produce the entire $10 million. If we used $500 thousand, we could produce $20 million and make up for the time factor involved.

Either way, despite the initial appearance of uninsurability and the fear of losing $10 million from his estate forever, surrogate planning would recover the estate tax loss and help ensure financial security for his heirs.

INSURANCE FOR THE UNINSURABLE

$20 Million Estate

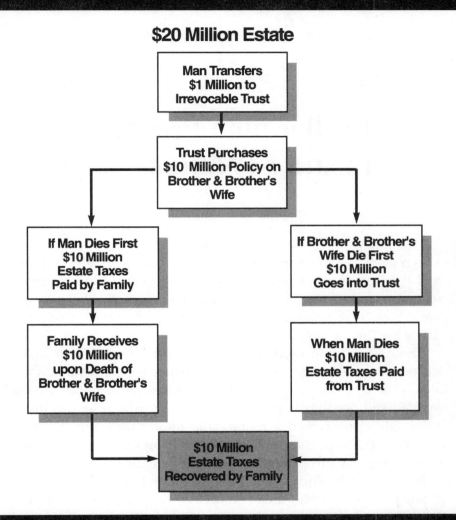

Man Transfers $1 Million to Irrevocable Trust

Trust Purchases $10 Million Policy on Brother & Brother's Wife

If Man Dies First $10 Million Estate Taxes Paid by Family

If Brother & Brother's Wife Die First $10 Million Goes into Trust

Family Receives $10 Million upon Death of Brother & Brother's Wife

When Man Dies $10 Million Estate Taxes Paid from Trust

$10 Million Estate Taxes Recovered by Family

SURROGATE INSURANCE PAYS $10 MILLION ESTATE TAX

All figures are based on current assumptions. Charts are for illustrative purposes only.
This illustration used a last-to-die insurance policy for a male and female both age 60.
©1994 WEALTH CREATION CENTERS℠ - Barry Kaye Associates

5

Reallocation Produces an Extra $3 Million—Free

I HAD CLIENTS who were in their late fifties. Six years ago, when we had first set about to purchase insurance as an estate planning tool, the man had been uninsurable due to a medical condition. We'd bought $8 million to cover their estate taxes using only the wife's life for the policy.

Though we often tend to think of health as something which starts out good and gets progressively worse with time, this is not always the case. Six years after the initial insurance purchase, the man's condition has improved to the point where he was insurable. And that created a remarkable opportunity which clearly illustrates the importance of re-evaluating your coverage as conditions in your health or financial status change.

In the six years since the original policy had been purchased on a one-pay basis, it had amassed a cash value of $750 thousand. Now the man was interested in a last-to-die policy because he had heard that the returns were better. Since the purpose of the insurance was to recover estate tax costs for his children, the couple didn't need insurance on only one of them. The proceeds wouldn't be used until after they were both dead and therefore they were excellent candidates for last-to-die coverage and the savings it presents.

We took the man's case to 5 insurance companies to see if they would accept him on a standard basis. (His wife remained in good health and was also given a standard rating.) Three of the companies agreed. (This serves to demonstrate the need for diversity. Not all insurance companies use the same basis for their ratings; had the man not applied to five different companies, had he limited his applications to the two which did not give him a standard rating, this program could not have been accomplished.)

By taking advantage of his improved health and transferring the $750 thousand existing cash value to a last-to-die policy, we were able to purchase $11 million worth of coverage at no additional cost to the couple on a one-pay basis, based on current assumptions. Since their original policy had been for $8 million, this new policy gave them an extra $3 million for free!

Additional conversations revealed that the couple's estate value was continuing to increase. They were both still young and anticipated that ultimately their estate tax costs would be considerably higher than they were right then. Knowing first hand that there was no time like the present, when both enjoyed good health and standard ratings, to make the insurance purchase which would cover the anticipated increase in insurance, they inquired about purchasing $5 million more. However, they were not sure they wanted to put up enough cash to buy this additional coverage on a one-pay basis.

It was revealed through our conversations that the couple had no leverage on their various stock holdings. I suggested they borrow $330 thousand from their current brokerage firm which offered broker call rates of 5%. The interest cost of this loan would be only $15 thousand a year and the $330 thousand borrowed amount would be sufficient to fully fund a $5 million last-to-die policy on a one-pay basis under current assumptions. In this manner, the minimal interest payment of $15,000 a year would purchase $5 million in additional coverage.

The end result was that the $15 thousand per year interest cost was the only added expense in increasing their total coverage from the $8 million of the original policy to $16 million—$11 million in the last-to-die policy which was purchased from the $750 thousand cash value transfer and an additional $5 million funded with the $15 thousand per year interest cost of leveraging their stocks. This may well have been the best investment he ever made at his stock brokerage firm.

FAMILY RECEIVES EXTRA $8 MILLION FOR $15,000 YEARLY

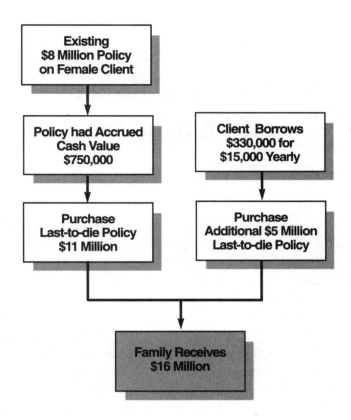

**Existing
$8 Million Policy
on Female Client**

**Policy had Accrued
Cash Value
$750,000**

**Client Borrows
$330,000 for
$15,000 Yearly**

**Purchase
Last-to-die Policy
$11 Million**

**Purchase
Additional $5 Million
Last-to-die Policy**

**Family Receives
$16 Million**

$8 MILLION BECOMES $16 MILLION FOR FAMILY

All figures are based on current assumptions. Charts are for illustrative purposes only.
This illustration used a last-to-die insurance policy for a male and female both age 55.
©1994 WEALTH CREATION CENTERS℠ - Barry Kaye Associates

6

Have Your Bagel
and Eat it, Too

THERE'S A BAGEL SHOP in Los Angeles owned by a delightful woman who is its heart. Her clientele comes as much because of her personal service and commitment as they do for her bagels. The continuing success of the business is predicated and relies upon her on-going involvement.

To keep the business healthy and create new growth, the woman needed to invest more capital. To raise the money, she considered selling a portion of the business. In that way, she could put more money into the business without depleting her own funds and create a more profitable venture for her children's future inheritance. But, splitting the profits with a partner would reduce her own income.

"What's your ultimate goal," I asked her, "how much are you looking to leave your children?"

"If I could accommodate this expansion," she replied, "the business could ultimately be worth another $2 million during my lifetime. But I don't know if my children could sell it for that much, or if it would produce income at that level, without me."

"So, best case, your children would have another $2 million. But in the meantime, your income will suffer because you'll have to share profits with a new investor/partner."

I then showed her how she could guarantee that the business would be "bought" for the additional $2 million after her death without current or future profits being depleted by a partner.

It wasn't necessary for the woman herself to increase the profitability of her business; she was really only interested in maximizing its value for her children. She had some excess cash flow from the business which she was planning to put into its expansion together with the money she thought to raise from an investor in order to greatly expand the business' worth. But, without her to personally manage the bagel shop, her investments might well prove to have limited lasting effectiveness.

I asked the woman how much money she had to put into the business. She told me there was about $30 thousand a year in "excess" income which she could afford to reinvest in the business without it hurting her lifestyle. I then showed her how that same $30 thousand per year could be used to purchase a life insurance policy which would produce the $2 million she desired for her children upon her death.

The benefits of the insurance method were extensive. The results were guaranteed since she would eventually die. There was no risk of the business not performing as hoped or of there not being enough time left for her to build it to its ultimate level; the policy would pay off whether she lived another thirty years or died the next day. There was also no concern about the business being devalued by the loss of her personal involvement. The policy purchase price would cost no more than she was already willing to put back into the business and, in fact, would leave her with more money since she wouldn't be splitting the profits with a partner.

Using the profits from the business, the woman could purchase her children's security at virtually no cost to her own lifestyle. Upon her death, they would receive a guaranteed additional $2 million and would have the choice of continuing the business and deriving additional income from it or selling it for whatever remaining value it had without their mother to run it. Basically, she would provide the bagels and the insurance would provide the cream . . . cheese.

HAVE YOUR BAGEL & EAT IT TOO

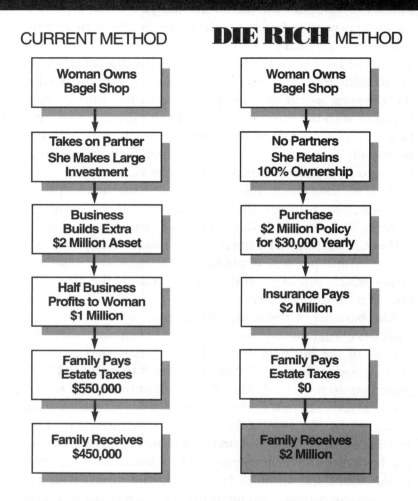

CURRENT METHOD

DIE RICH METHOD

CURRENT METHOD	DIE RICH METHOD
Woman Owns Bagel Shop	Woman Owns Bagel Shop
Takes on Partner She Makes Large Investment	No Partners She Retains 100% Ownership
Business Builds Extra $2 Million Asset	Purchase $2 Million Policy for $30,000 Yearly
Half Business Profits to Woman $1 Million	Insurance Pays $2 Million
Family Pays Estate Taxes $550,000	Family Pays Estate Taxes $0
Family Receives $450,000	Family Receives $2 Million

WHY RISK CAPITAL & SPLIT PROFITS? THERE'S MORE DOUGH IN INSURANCE

7

$4 Million
From $150 Thousand

Many people shy away from discussions about life insurance because of one fact it can make painfully clear—the fact of death. Neither the life insurance industry nor I created the fact of death in order to use it to sell product. Death comes to us all. But I have always believed that anything a person can do to make the painful fact of death a little less hurtful, any triumph we can take from its final defeat, eases the passage a little.

I have repeated over and over that life must always come first. That the living should never sacrifice one bit of their own security or happiness for those that will come after. Life is too short and too important to spend it focusing on death. But I also believe that, if the means are available to do so without sacrifice, leaving the best legacy you can after your death enhances life.

The following story includes a sad ending. As, unfortunately, everyone's story does. But I am including it anyway, not to exploit the pain of death, but to demonstrate the power of life.

A man came to me who had $500 thousand of insurance on his wife. He said it was his intent to use some additional monies he had to buy another $500 thousand on her to achieve a desired $1 million in total coverage. I showed him how he could use the cash value which had built up in the policy, along with the additional funds he'd already earmarked for the second $500 thousand policy and, keeping the same premium payments, purchase $2 million instead of $1 million.

I consulted with the man and his attorney and showed them exactly how the optimizing would occur. Finally, with the consent of his lawyer, he decided to consummate the transaction and purchased the $2 million of coverage.

A very short time later, the man's wife became ill (had he waited, it would have been too late—she would have been uninsurable). Then she died. It may seem callous to point out that, though considerably fewer premium payments than planned had been made, the insurance still paid the whole $2 million, thereby increasing the return many times from the less than $150,000 of total premiums paid from the very beginning. I do so only to demonstrate the single most important benefit of insurance. The fact is, none of us knows or can predict how long we will live. Only insurance can provide the certainty that, whenever death comes, your result is guaranteed. If it seems a cold fact, it is certainly no more cold than the irrefutable fact that death will come.

The man was, of course, devastated by the loss of his wife. No amount of money could possibly replace her or return the joy of her to his life. All he wanted now, was to take care of his children . . . to make sure that, when he died, they would at least be freed from financial concerns while coping with their loss and grief. There is some comfort in that, he knew. Families devastated by financial difficulties after the death of a breadwinner have an added tragedy to endure and he wanted to spare his children that hardship.

Though the man was quite old himself and not in the best of health, we were able to use the $2 million he had received from the insurance company upon his wife's death to purchase a $4 million policy on him for his children's benefit.

Now, his children will eventually receive $4 million instead of $500 thousand—accomplished with practically no additional cost from the existing $500 thousand policy other than the initial premiums of less than $150,000. It won't replace their parents, but it will provide a legacy of their love and it will help free them from much of the financial distress that often accompanies death. It can be used to discount estate tax costs, to save family property from liquidation, to retain the family business and/or to provide needed income.

TOMORROW MAY NEVER COME

Client owns $500,000 Policy on his Wife

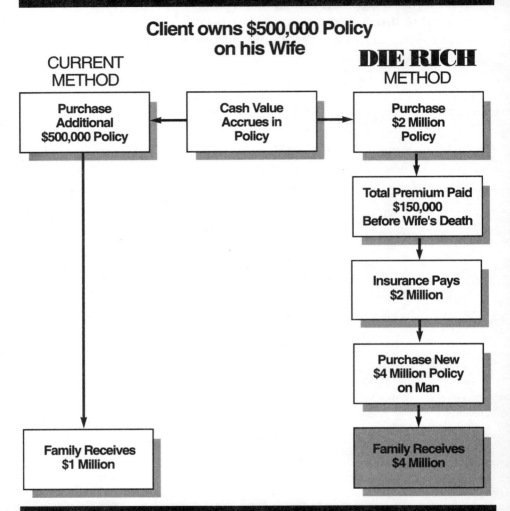

CURRENT METHOD

DIE RICH METHOD

Purchase Additional $500,000 Policy

Cash Value Accrues in Policy

Purchase $2 Million Policy

Total Premium Paid $150,000 Before Wife's Death

Insurance Pays $2 Million

Purchase New $4 Million Policy on Man

Family Receives $1 Million

Family Receives $4 Million

$150,000 PRODUCES $4 MILLION TAX FREE!

All figures are based on current assumptions. Charts are for illustrative purposes only.
This illustration used an individual insurance policy for a male age 78 and a female age 70.
©1994 WEALTH CREATION CENTERS℠ - Barry Kaye Associates

8

Maximizing Munis

I HAD A CLIENT who had $1.5 million in municipal bonds as part of his $10 million portfolio. The yields were going down so he would only be making 5% or 6% and, more importantly, he didn't need any of the income whatsoever. Ultimately, the tax free income the bonds earned would just effectively accrue to his principal and be taxed at his death at 55 cents on the dollar.

I showed him a $5 million last-to-die policy which, based on his and his wife's age and the current assumptions of interest and mortality, would produce a 3 to 1 return of $5 million for $1.5 million. There was no way that the $1.5 million in municipal bonds could ever hope to create a comparable return. And, in fact, the $1.5 million of bonds would only be worth $750 thousand upon their deaths after estate taxes were collected.

Utilizing the approach I recommended, and applying the couple's $600 thousand exemptions along with their annual $10 thousand exclusions, they would be able to avoid all taxes thus producing $5 million for their family not in contrast to $1.5 million, but, in actuality, in contrast to $750 thousand.

But even if the couple had used up their $600 thousand exemptions, the only extra expense would have been the gift taxes of $750 thousand on the $1.5 million transfer of the bond value to the trust to purchase the insurance. This $750 thousand, coupled with the premium costs of $1.5 million would result in a total cost of $2.25 million. If that $2.25 million had remained in their estate, it would have been taxed upon their deaths and their children would only have been left with $1.1 million instead of the $5 million using the approach I suggested would produce. I asked again, as I have so many times, "Why purchase an investment in the hopes it will triple its value, when that value will ultimately be halved by estate taxes? You already have the tripling capacity in your portfolio using a life insurance policy that is guaranteed to pay off, tax free to your heirs, when you die, whether that's tomorrow or 25 years from now."

There was an interesting twist to this specific situation. At the time we put the plan together, the man was unsure who he wanted to leave the proceeds from the insurance to—his heirs, his favorite charity or his own foundation. He decided to keep the money in his estate until he could make a designation and so did not transfer the ownership of the policy.

If he decided to give the policy to charity, the whole $1.5 million premium or the cash value would count as an income tax deduction for his wife and no gift taxes would be due upon the transfer as the charity is exempt. If he chose to leave it to his heirs but did not transfer it to a trust before his death, it would be subject to estate taxes which would deplete it by half. Even so, his children would still receive $2.5 million instead of the original $750 thousand they would have gotten had he left the money in the municipal bonds.

As it happens, recently the man called me and stated that he would like to transfer the policy out of his estate. I am working on various options that will avoid the most taxes on a legal basis for the benefit of all concerned. One method being considered utilizes a charity approach which would ultimately serve not only his own objectives but benefit the American public and the government. This method of gifting to charity offsets the need for further taxation in order for the government to support social institutions.

One final point. This policy was bought at higher interest assumptions. The client may need an additional 4 yearly payments of $142 thousand eventually if interest rates don't rise. This still may not be necessary depending upon his situation, however, even if he pays the extra money, it is only equivalent to $257 thousand after taxes. The $5 million will still cost only a little more than $2 million.

MAXIMIZING MUNIS

CURRENT METHOD   **DIE RICH** METHOD

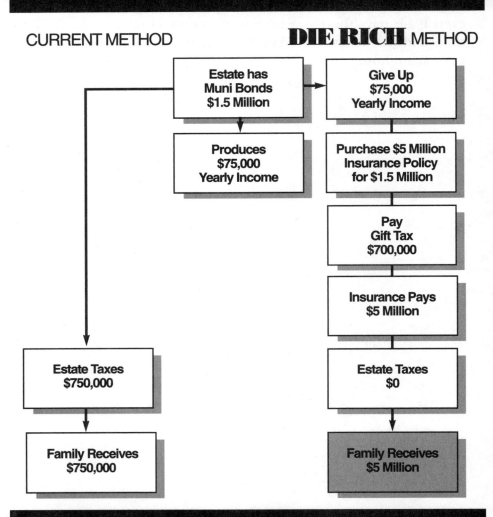

$75,000 YEARLY INCOME CREATES $5 MILLION

All figures are based on current assumptions. Charts are for illustrative purposes only.
This illustration used a last-to-die insurance policy for a male and female both age 78.
©1994 WEALTH CREATION CENTERS℠ - Barry Kaye Associates

9

Turning $148 Thousand Into $3 Million Tax Free and a $1.9 Million Estate Into $5.9 Million After Taxes

A CLIENT CAME TO ME who was interested in covering the estate taxes of $1.1 million on his $3 million estate. He had a rolled-over IRA with approximately $463 thousand in it. I showed him that the IRA would only be worth $148 thousand at his death after his children paid income and estate taxes on it. He was surprised to learn what the retirement account was really worth and since he didn't need the asset to support his lifestyle, he asked me if there wasn't something better he could be doing with the money.

I suggested he close out and distribute the IRA and pay the 28% income tax which would be due of $130 thousand (1991 maximum tax bracket) and then transfer the remaining $330 thousand to an irrevocable trust. Since the $330 thousand was within his $600 thousand allowable exemption, there would be no transfer tax. In turn, the $300 thousand would buy $3 million of life insurance for the ultimate benefit of his children. My client was delighted to learn that, without any additional cash outlay, he could effectively turn $148 thousand after taxes into $3 million with no taxes—an increase of more than 20 times and a total doubling of his gross estate.

Having about $30 thousand left from the distribution of the IRA, the couple decided to add to it from the principal they had, which was still well in excess of their needs. For an additional $70 thousand, making $100 thousand total, they purchased a $1 million policy to be distributed among their nine grandchildren so that each grandchild would receive approximately $110 thousand.

Without any great outlay of additional capital, except for $70 thousand of discretionary money, the couple had accomplished more than they had dreamed of. Though their $3 million estate would still lose $1.1 million to estate taxation, their children would receive the full $3 million from the insurance company for a total of $4.9 million—not only had they recovered the estate tax loss, they had surpassed it. In addition, an extra million had been created to gift to the grandchildren.

Without this plan, the IRA would only have been worth $148 thousand and his $3 million estate after taxes would have been worth only $1.9 million for his heirs. With it, a total of $5.9 million is realized and the couple enjoys the emotional benefit of knowing they have optimized their money beyond any imagined potential for the good of their children and grandchildren.

TURN $148,000 INTO $3 MILLION

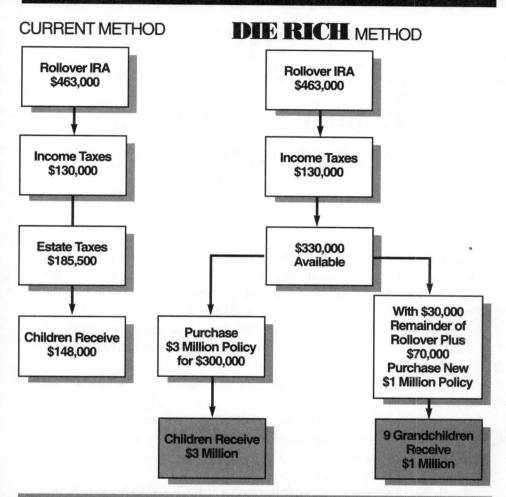

CURRENT METHOD

DIE RICH METHOD

Rollover IRA
$463,000

Rollover IRA
$463,000

Income Taxes
$130,000

Income Taxes
$130,000

Estate Taxes
$185,500

$330,000
Available

Children Receive
$148,000

Purchase
$3 Million Policy
for $300,000

With $30,000
Remainder of
Rollover Plus
$70,000
Purchase New
$1 Million Policy

Children Receive
$3 Million

9 Grandchildren
Receive
$1 Million

Original Gross Estate $3 Million - Net Estate $1.9 Million

DIE RICH METHOD NET ESTATE $5.9 MILLION

All figures are based on current assumptions. Charts are for illustrative purposes only.
This illustration used a last-to-die insurance policy for a male and female both age 60.
©1994 WEALTH CREATION CENTERS℠ - Barry Kaye Associates

10

A Combination of Benefits
Made to Order

OFTEN, I AM CONTACTED by accountants, financial advisors or attorneys on behalf of their clients who are looking to incorporate some of my capital optimizing strategies into their clients' planning. The following letter, reprinted, for obvious reasons without using any of the names involved, is a recent example of an inquiry which incorporated many of the different opportunities I recommend.

The couple for whom the inquiry was made—I'll call them Bob and Betty—enjoyed an average age of 80 at the time this correspondence was taking place. This letter represents the culmination of numerous conversations aimed at fully understanding Bob's and Betty's goals and presenting them with the various options available to fulfill them.

"In accordance with our discussion, I have spoken to Bob and Betty in order to fully understand their objectives. This letter will outline my concepts within the confines of those objectives.

"Utilizing an immediate annuity based on the lives of both Bob and Betty, it is possible to optimize their current returns substantially beyond what their municipal bonds are now producing. The annuities would be purchased from a "AAA" Standard & Poors rated and an A.M. Best A+ rated old life insurance company. The annuities would be guaranteed for the rest of their lives by the consortium of insurance companies we will use. It is important to note that the annuities represent a return of principal and interest; using them will substantially increase Bob's and Betty's yearly cash flow but will eliminate the principal that was used to purchase the annuity.

"An immediate annuity purchased on Bob's life alone would produce annual, after-tax income of approximately $153 thousand (15.3%) for as long as Bob was alive.

"Purchased on Betty's life alone, the annuity would produce approximately $140 thousand (14%) after taxes for the rest of her life.

"If we used a joint and survivorship immediate annuity, the annual after-tax return would be about $117 thousand (11.6%). The benefit of this type of annuity is that it continues to pay its return on a guaranteed basis throughout the lives of both spouses.

"Since Bob and Betty are currently earning 7% on the municipal bonds they own and since many of those bonds are being called and the new bond purchases being made to replace them are only providing a 5% return, the immediate annuity represents a significant increase.

"Using these annuities, we can either increase Bob's and Betty's yield substantially, make money available for their children or grandchildren for the purpose of paying their estate taxes or increase the overall inheritance they leave. They have stated that they already feel they have sufficiently taken care of charity through their donations of art and the transfer of the $5 million of existing insurance on their lives to their charitable foundation. Any additional monies which we create they feel should go for the benefit of their children.

"Following are several outlines for programs which could be used to accomplish their objective:

"1. Bob and Betty wish to make the beneficiary of their existing $5 million last-to-die policy their charitable foundation. This can be accomplished by naming the "Foundation" the irrevocable beneficiary thus providing a tax deductible expense at this time. An alternative would be to transfer the ownership of the policy as well as the beneficiary to the foundation. This also results in a tax deductible contribution in accordance with appropriate tax law. However, I understand that they do not need these additional tax deductions and, more importantly, Betty has indicated that she does not want to give up ownership of the policy as she would like to control the cash value it contains as an emergency asset, so I am not recommending this course at this time.

"2. They can change the beneficiary to the foundation now but retain the ownership. They will not receive an income tax deduction, but the $5 million will be removed from their estate at the time of their deaths when the charity receives the policy proceeds, in accordance with their objectives. More importantly, they will retain the ownership of the policy during their lives thus allowing them access to the cash values should the need arise and providing the ability to change the beneficiary should they so desire. I do recommend this course of action at this time as it fully addresses both their concerns and objectives.

"3. Bob and Betty could optimize their municipal bond money by purchasing one of the immediate annuities discussed earlier securing 11.6% to 15.3% yearly guaranteed after tax income for the rest of their lives based on current taxes and life expectancies and depending on which annuity they chose (Bob, Betty or Joint and Survivor). This could double their annual income from the current new municipal bonds being purchased at 5% or 6%. Since they have approximately $8 million in muni bonds, it would only require a $4 million immediate annuity to produce the exact same after tax income.

"4. There will be $4 million left in municipal bonds after we put $4 million into the immediate annuity to produce the same income Bob and Betty currently receive from their $8 million of munis. This can be used to create additional tax free income for them, or the funds could be utilized to purchase additional annuities with the greater return and the resulting doubling of their annual tax free income. However, municipal bonds are liquid and annuities are not. Once you purchase the annuity, the principal no longer exists for you; only the income is guaranteed. Therefore, understanding the concerns of Bob and Betty, my recommendation would be that, if you utilize this approach, you purchase no more than $4 million of annuities, thus retaining the remaining $4 million with excess income beyond what they use and maintain complete liquidity.

"One additional point. The purchase of $4 million of annuities will eliminate that $4 million from their estate resulting in a savings of approximately $2.2 million in estate taxes for their family.

"Two final options exist:

"5. Since $4 million in immediate annuities can produce the same income as $8 million in municipal bonds, Bob and Betty could use part or all of the remaining $4 million to optimize their income tax free and estate tax free gifts to their children and/or grandchildren. Based on their last policy and their current age, they could purchase additional insurance at the rate of approximately 2.5 to 1. In other words, they could utilize approximately $2 million to purchase an additional $5 million of insurance for the benefit of their children or grandchildren. In order to avoid estate taxes on the $5 million of proceeds, they would pay a gift tax of approximately $800 thousand on the $2 million transferred to the life insurance company based on current assumptions. This policy can be purchased on Bob and/or Betty depending upon the outcome of the medical results at this time. There are new techniques which could possibly allow us to purchase additional insurance, with no additional outlay, if their health was not good as it was when we originally initiated the existing policy.

"6. There is one final outstanding approach used by people with substantial assets such as Bob and Betty. I am referring to a generation skipping trust for the grandchildren. As you are aware, they can each give $1 million to the grandchildren with no generation skipping transfer tax. Some of the principal (up to $2 million) that we made available with the purchase of annuities could be used for insurance on Bob and Betty.

Once again, for the benefit of their grandchildren, the $2 million would produce approximately $5 million if used to purchase a policy on Bob and Betty. But, if they wished to optimize their money completely, they could use as little as $500 thousand (up to $2 million) gifted to the generation skipping trust to purchase insurance on the grandchildren's parents, Bob's and Betty's children. Obviously, the leverage at their ages is much more substantial than the 2.5 to 1 return available on Bob and Betty. In this manner, depending upon the children's ages, they could produce approximately a 40 to 1 return of $20 million in the trust for the grandchildren upon the death of their children. The numbers become so enormous, you could utilize smaller amounts and still accomplish tremendous results (i.e. $100 thousand on last-to-die on the children produces $4 million tax free ultimately for the grandchildren). Bob and Betty explored this possibility last year. In other words, $100 thousand for each grandchild totalling $400 thousand would produce approximately $16 million total in a dynasty generation skipping trust.

"These figures can be adjusted to accommodate their objectives. Obviously, any additional money spent or transferred to the children, or grandchildren, would not impact Bob and Betty, as we have doubled their income with the annuities or utilized only half as much principal to produce the same income thus freeing the money for any strategy among those described above."

MBA COMBINATION PLATE
$4 MILLION SERVED 4 DIFFERENT WAYS

Option A	Option B	Option C	Option D
Client Owns $4 Million in Muni Bonds Yields 6% Yearly	Purchase $4 Million Annuity Yields 11.6%-15.3% Yearly	Purchase $2 Million Annuity Yields 11.6%-15.3% Yearly	Purchase $4 Million Annuity Yields 11.6%-15.3% Yearly
Munis Produce $240,000 Yearly Income	Annuity Produces $600,000 Yearly Income	Annuity Produces $300,000 Yearly Income	Annuity Produces $600,000 Yearly Income Retain $240,000
		Purchase $5 Million Policy on Couple with Remaining $2 Million	Purchase $60 Million 7-Pay Policy on Children for $360,000 Yearly
Estate Tax $2.2 Million	Removes $4 Million From Estate - Estate Tax $0	Estate Tax $0	Estate Tax $0
Costs Family $2.2 Million in Estate Taxes	Saves Family $2.2 Million in Estate Taxes	Children Receive $5 Million	Grandchildren Receive $60 Million

All figures are based on current assumptions, current taxes and life expectancy and ability to secure coverage. Charts are for illustrative purposes only. This illustration used a last-to-die insurance policy for a male and female both age 80.

©1994 WEALTH CREATION CENTERS℠ - Barry Kaye Associates

11

A Legacy of Love

An ELDERLY COUPLE, who had made ample provisions for their own children, was anxious to make additional provisions for their grandchildren. They had a comfortable estate which produced some excess income. They had used a portion of the surplus to purchase insurance on themselves for the benefit of their children to be used to recover the anticipated estate taxes. Now they had just enough left that they could each afford to use their $10 thousand annual tax free gifts on behalf of each of their five grandchildren and they wanted to know how they could best optimize that amount.

I showed the couple four ways in which to significantly leverage their $10 thousand annual tax free gifts.

The first plan involved using an annuity whereby they would gift $20 thousand (their combined $10 thousand gifts) to each grandchild. There would be no gift tax and they would reduce their estate by that amount. The grandchild would purchase an annuity with an interest rate of 7.5%; projecting that rate forward, each grandchild would have approximately $41 thousand in the 10th year, $85 thousand in the 20th year and $417 thousand by the time they reached age 60. At that point, the money can then become a monthly annuity for the rest of the grandchild's life of $2,830 each and every month.

The second program involved gifting each grandchild with $20 thousand each year for 10 years. The $20 thousand was coming from excess income so, in all likelihood, it would be available each year. By the end of ten years, there would be $200 thousand gifted to each grandchild which, at current projected interest rates of 7.5% would have earned an additional $104 thousand making for a combined total of $304 thousand. In the 20th year, interest income would have increased the $200 thousand to $627 thousand and, by the 27th year, at which time the couple's oldest grandchild would be 44, it would be worth $1 million. By the time the grandchild reached age 60, the $200 thousand would have increased to over $3 million and would be producing monthly income of approximately $20 thousand. A lifetime of financial security would be provided from the same $20 thousand annual gifts.

Using the third program, the grandparents would gift $20 thousand for one year to their grandchild who, in turn, would purchase a policy on his father and mother (age 60) which would ultimately produce approximately $200 thousand. Whether the father and mother die the next day or 40 years later, the grandchild will receive a guaranteed $200 thousand income and estate tax free. Of course, this same program would be initiated for each of the grandchildren returning the similar result based on their parents' ages.

Each of these programs would accomplish the goal of optimizing the annual gifts and providing financial security for the couple's grandchildren. But the fourth program is the one I most strongly recommended.

Using the son who was 47 at the time and had the grandchild who was 16 as an example, I suggested the couple use the $20 thousand annual gift to pay for a 7-pay insurance premium on a policy which would produce a return of $1.2 million. Whether their grandson's father died the next day or 40 years later, the grandson would receive a guaranteed $1.2 million. And again, this program could be duplicated for each of the couple's grandchildren.

By following this program, the couple would have reduced their estate $140 thousand over the 7 years for each of the grand-children they gifted. The net cost then would really be only $63 thousand as this is the amount that would have been left of the $140 thousand after estate taxes were paid on it had it not been transferred out of the estate before their deaths. In effect, the couple would have transferred $1.2 million after all taxes to their grandchild at a cost of only $63 thousand.

If they implemented the program for each of their five grand-children, the yearly cost would be $100 thousand ($20 thousand each) transferred gift tax free to the grandchildren to purchase $1.2 million for each. The end result over a 7 year period would be a total outlay of $700 thousand ($100 thousand annually) based on current assumptions which, if it hadn't been transferred out of their estate, would have been subject to estate taxes of $385 thousand leaving the family only $315 thousand. So $315 thousand produces a cumulative benefit ultimately of $6 million ($1.2 million for each of five grandchildren) income and estate tax free.

As an additional benefit, the cash value after the total payments of $140 thousand in the tenth year would be $152 thousand. At the end of 20 years, it will be $291 thousand and at the end of 30 years cash values will exceed $475 thousand. And, after 40 years, the cash value will be $685 thousand. The death benefit remains $1.2 million whenever death were to occur. But during the years before that sad eventuality, the policy is still an important asset and the couple's grandchildren can borrow against it at anytime should they have need of the money for an emergency.

In a simple and guaranteed fashion, the couple could choose any one of 4 different plans each of which will maximize their gifts to the grandchildren and create a legacy of love to protect and provide for them.

LEGACY OF LOVE

Option A	Option B	Option C	Option D
Give Combined $20,000 Annual Tax Free Gift to Grandchild for for 1 Year	Give Combined $20,000 Annual Tax Free Gift to Grandchild for 10 Years	Give Combined $20,000 Annual Tax Free Gift to Grandchild for 1 Year	Give Combined $20,000 Annual Tax Free Gift to Grandchild for 7 Years
Grandchild Purchases Annuity	Grandchild Purchases Annuity	Grandchild Purchases 1-Pay $200,000 Policy on his Parents	Grandchild Purchases 7-Pay $1,200,000 Policy on his Parents
Grandchild's Assets $41,000 Year 10 $85,000 Year 20 $417,000 Age 60	Grandchild's Assets $304,000 Year 10 $627,000 Year 20 $3 Million Age 60		
Produces $2,830 Monthly for Life	Produces $20,000 Monthly for Life	Grandchild Receives $200,000 at Parents Death	Grandchild Receives $1,200,000 at Parents Death

MAXIMIZE YOUR GIFTS TO YOUR GRANDCHILDREN

All figures are based on current assumptions. Charts are for illustrative purposes only.

©1994 WEALTH CREATION CENTERS℠ - Barry Kaye Associates

247

12

A Potpourri of Persuasions

DURING MY OVER THIRTY YEAR CAREER, I have heard many of the same arguments against life insurance over and over again. To this day, most of them make no real sense. I think they are used as an excuse not to face up to the underlying guarantee which makes insurance such an invaluable financial tool—the guarantee of death. And, while I can certainly understand the desire to avoid having to face the reality of death, it is an unavoidable tragedy. The tragedy of estate decimation due to estate taxes is completely avoidable and it has always been my belief that, since you can't avoid the one, you really should avoid compounding it with the other.

Following are a few brief replies to the excuses and arguments I often hear. If you hear your own voice in any of the examples, please listen carefully to my answer—it can mean so much to your posterity and isn't it really through them that we all live forever. Insurance discussions needn't be about death and dying. In estate planning it is about embracing the lives to come.

❧ Advice is Cheap; Estate Taxes Aren't. "My Advisor Says No."

Once you have amassed an estate big enough to require estate tax planning, you probably have a number of advisors whose assistance you rely on in determining the best course. Unfortunately, these professionals do not include among their references a crystal ball. They aren't always right and they aren't always as knowledgeable as they think they are. The following story illustrates this point:

It seems that about 15 years ago, Kenneth Langone offered Ross Perot a 70% stake in the new business he was starting—a chain of discount hardware stores called Home Depot. The asking price for the 70% Perot was offered was $2 million. On the advice of one of his financial advisors, Perot demurred.

Today, a 70% share in Home Depot would be worth over $12 billion! That's a 6,000 times increase.

Obviously, advisors do make mistakes. Big ones. Don't let their errors become yours. The stakes may not be as big in terms of money, but in terms of your children's futures they are immeasurable. Even the top advisors (we assume Perot had access to the best) don't know everything. And, when it comes to insurance as an estate tax planning tool, unfortunately many of them don't know nearly enough.

How Much is Enough? "What Guarantees The Best Return?"

Often I have clients or prospects similar to a man who visited me the other day who see the merit of the concepts I espouse and have the money or leverage to implement them, but who wonder why they should spend the money to leave their children even more. Many of them feel that, as they had started with nothing and accomplished so much, their children have already been given enough advantages.

Naturally, this decision is up to the individual. If they really feel that they don't want to provide any more for their children than they already have, and they really understand that what they will ultimately leave after estate taxes is less than half of what they've amassed, then that is fine.

But I always wonder why it is that these people single out life insurance as the one investment tool which is thought about in this manner.

These same people continue to make their stock investments, they continue to purchase real estate, they continue to seek out every other means of optimizing their money during their lifetime. Why do they do this? Most of them have more than enough principal to support their own lifestyles. Surely they understand that any additional earnings will accrue for the benefit of their children. Yet they have just stated that they think their children are already sufficiently provided for. And still, the psychological/philosophical question of whether their children will have too much money never occurs to them in the context of these other investments.

I can only conclude that they are victims of the denial and lack of rational thinking which surrounds the subject of life insurance. Since the life insurance investment will impact their lives in exactly the same fashion as all their other investment vehicles, I can think of no other distinction.

If, in truth, these people feel they have reached a limit in what they want to leave to their children, then I suggest they protect their assets for the good of their favorite charity. Why would anyone choose to give more than half of everything they've spent a lifetime amassing in one lump sum benefit to the government when they could, instead, replace the tax loss and provide, in addition to the lump sum tax payment, an ongoing legacy of societal benefits?

❧ The Cobbler's Children Go Barefoot

It is said that an attorney who represents himself has a fool for a client.

I had an attorney come to me who wanted to purchase insurance but felt he knew everything he needed to know to make his own decision about how to proceed. In effect he wanted me to be an "order taker" and just sell him the product he'd already decided he wanted. He couldn't be bothered with any advice from me on what he really needed.

Though I had grave trepidations about the man's planned course of action, he assured me he knew what he was doing and had his reasons for doing it that way.

Within 5 years, both the man and his wife were dead. The forced liquidation of his estate that ensued in order to meet the estate tax bill created havoc for his family. It would have been so simple to avoid this tragedy if he would only have allowed me to do the job I have trained over 30 years to do. I don't practice law, and, unfortunately, he was not as qualified to practice insurance planning as he thought he was.

I do not include this sad tale out of bitterness or spite. I do not mean to insult any member of any profession. But there is a point I must make and this story makes it best: like those in any other field, the nuances of life insurance as an estate tax planning vehicle are complex and involved. Don't have a fool for a client, enlist the aid of a knowledgeable professional.

℅. Preconception Deception

The revolution in life insurance is relatively recent and a lot of people haven't yet come to understand the changes and their advantages. Surprisingly, I find evidence of old thinking extremely prevalent in the one place I would think to avoid it—within the members of my own industry. But preconceptions also exist in sufficient numbers among laypeople to make it important to mention here.

All too often people come to me, or I have to deal with some insurance industry chairman or professional, who are holding on to old ways of thinking about insurance. No matter how much I show them the benefits of insurance products in estate planning, I can not get past their preconceived ideas that insurance is a necessary evil you buy against the tragic possibility of an early death.

There is so much more which today's insurance products can do, as I hope the pages of this book have amply demonstrated. It is such a shame when people fail to see what is right there in front of them and, as a result, their families suffer financial reversals which need never have occurred. These, truly, are the biggest victims of conventional wisdom.

&. Death Won't Wait

I can't tell you how often it happens that people who have come to me for a proposal initiate half of what their situation really needs or will need and then come back years later wanting to implement the rest. Unfortunately, in many instances, while they were waiting to make their decision, age and illness caught up with them. Now, they are uninsurable or the return they can earn on the insurance purchase has decreased substantially.

You pay for insurance with money but you buy it with good health. You'll never be younger or, in most cases, in better health than you are the first day you determine to make an insurance purchase. You'll never receive a better insurance value than when you are at your youngest and healthiest. And, while you can always cut back if you feel you have bought too much, there's no guarantee that you'll ever be healthy enough—or even alive—to buy more.

Life insurance has traditionally been thought of as a means to a solitary end. It was simply protection against the financial toll death takes on a family and was most commonly purchased on the major breadwinner to help provide for his spouse and children in the event of his sudden absence.

The programs detailed in this book are based on a different way of thinking about life insurance.

Whether purchased for the standard goal of providing necessary funds for a family following the loss of a provider, or utilized in the many ways shown here to discount estate tax costs or create and preserve wealth, life insurance is, in reality, the ultimate loving gift. Protecting your loved ones' financial welfare, ensuring that their lives are enriched by financial security, allowing them the freedom to pursue their dreams unfettered by financial necessity—what greater, more lasting, gift can you give? Only the gift of your love . . . and isn't a lifetime of security and freedom the ultimate expression of that love?

Following are four examples of what can be accomplished when life insurance is looked at in this new manner; when it is thought of as a gift of love, a gift that lasts beyond a lifetime.

1. I have one client who continually sees that he can optimize his insurance. His existing cash values are huge but are never utilized to their total capacity. No matter what I show him and no matter how much he buys, he keeps coming up with new money instead of utilizing his policies and optimizing the end result. His potential for creating additional money at no cost is on-going and a great source of frustration to me. But, because he was thinking of life insurance in traditional manners, I could never get him to understand that there were better ways. Until I discussed with him the concept of life insurance as being the ultimate gift. Suddenly, he had a whole new perspective.

He said he had friends and employees he always wanted to take care of and he thought this was the ideal solution. He immediately purchased 10 policies to be gifted to these people as a gesture of his caring and appreciation and—finally—he is going to use some of his existing money to pay for them. Somehow, the simplicity of the gift concept made the entire opportunity for optimization easier for him to grasp. Life insurance is the ultimate gift.

2. I was sitting at my barber's talking to the man in the next chair about my belief that life insurance represents the ultimate gift. My manicurist overheard our conversation and stated that she had saved over $100 thousand during her lifetime. She had two children and wanted to leave them each $100 thousand upon her death. She had never considered life insurance before, it had seemed something that was beyond her means and inappropriate to her desires. But she was intrigued with the idea of a loving,

lasting gift and said she would gladly spend $20 thousand on a one-payment basis to purchase two gift policies that would provide $100 thousand each for her two children. As simply as that, a concept had been clarified for her that would enable her to accomplish her goal. Her happy reaction reaffirmed my previous thoughts that there are too many people intimidated by the complexity of insurance who could surely benefit from it if its benefits and presentation could only be simplified. Life insurance is the ultimate gift.

3. A family member had joined one his relatives in an investment which ultimately failed. The relative, my client, had always felt badly and was concerned about the loss that was incurred by this member of his family. While my client's relative understood the possibility of loss when he went into the investment, and while he never held a grudge about it, my client still felt badly. When I mentioned in passing to him that I had begun to realize that life insurance truly represented the ultimate gift one person could make to another, he suddenly saw the perfect way to make amends. He'd never considered life insurance as a means of payback before, but now he decided to purchase a policy on his relative's lives for the benefit of their grandchildren. In this manner, the $100 thousand loss was replaced for a cost of $10 thousand and my client was delighted to have made good on his bad investment advice. This truly was the ultimate gift to his relative.

4. Once I had realized the gift potential of life insurance, I saw for myself, as well as for others, the numerous opportunities for its use. I decided to make a gift to the American College of Life Underwriters (CLU) in Bryn Mawr, Pennsylvania. It was my way of paying back an industry that had produced so much for me and my family. What manner of repayment could be more appropriate than a gift which maximized my donation through the power of life insurance? Another use of life insurance, the ultimate gift.

It is obvious that numerous circumstances which previously were not thought of as being appropriately resolved through the purchase of life insurance can now be seen as benefitting greatly from this dynamic source of leverage. What previously was a product used only to insure against tragedy has now become a means of showing love and appreciation in highly optimized amounts for anyone in any situation.

Part Three

GLOSSARY

Average Age: This term is used when purchasing last-to-die, survivorship policies which base their premium rates and death benefits on the combined actuarial average of the ages of both husband and wife as opposed to one or the other.

Based on Current Assumptions: Insurance policy premiums are based on assumptions of mortality, expense and interest. These assumptions allow the insurance company to calculate how much premium is needed to provide the desired death benefit. Should changes occur in the basic assumptions after you have purchased your policy it could result either in additional or less premium payments or higher or lower premiums.

Based on Current Taxes: When quoting tax deductions or immediate annuities, all figures used are based upon current income tax laws. Any changes in those laws will impact the calculation of yields, producing higher or lower figures depending on the specific change in the tax laws.

Based on Life Expectancy: Annuities pay income based on both principal and interest. When calculating the income tax liability for annuities, there is a set amount of time during which taxes

257

are assessed only on the interest income portion of the total income. This period of time corresponds with the general life expectancy of the annuitant(s). Following that period of time, annuitant(s) will be taxed on the entire income.

Beneficiary: Refers to the person, or charity, who is designated to receive the death benefit of an insurance policy or the assets of a trust.

Call Rates: Brokers of stocks and bonds may lend you money against the value of your portfolio and in so doing will charge you interest based on the current call rate for the loan. Usually this rate is less than rates available through banks or lending institutions.

Cash Values: When the premium payments made on an insurance policy exceed the amount needed to support the death benefit, the resultant over-payment accrues as cash values within the policy. These cash values may be borrowed against or used to pay increased premiums required by a change in the assumptions which determined the original premium amounts. They may also be used to fund additional death benefits.

Charitable Foundation: In instances where you are gifting significant sums to charity, it may be beneficial to establish a charitable foundation. This is an institution which you would create by donation of funds and which would then exist to maintain and distribute income from those funds on an annual basis.

Charitable Gift Annuity: The donor transfers the asset directly to the charity in exchange for the charity's agreement to pay a lifetime annuity.

Charitable Lead Trusts: The Charitable Income or Lead Trust is the reverse of the Charitable Remainder Trust. The income interest is assigned to the charity, usually for a period of years and then the remainder generally passes to the donor's heirs. The amount of the estate tax deduction and the amount left for the heirs will depend upon the number of years and percentages of the annual payments and the investment results of the trustee.

Charitable Remainder Annuity Trust: A Charitable Remainder Annuity Trust (CRAT) is an irrevocable trust which pays a fixed dollar amount each year to a beneficiary such as the donor of the trust assets, his or her spouse, child, etc.

After the death of the income beneficiaries or at the end of a set number of years, whatever assets remain in the trust are distributed to the charities named in the trust.

If additional contributions are desired in later years, new trusts must be established.

Charitable Remainder Pooled Income Trust: Assets are transferred to a fund maintained by the charity. The fund then pays an agreed upon percentage each year for the life of the donor (and spouse). Payments can increase or decrease with the investment performance of the fund.

Charitable Remainder Unitrust: A Charitable Remainder Unitrust (CRUT) is an irrevocable trust which pays a fixed percentage of the value of its holdings each year to a beneficiary, such as the donor of the trust assets, his or her spouse, child, etc.

After the death of the income beneficiaries or at the end of a set number of years, whatever assets remain in the trust are distributed to the charities named in the trust.

Assets must be revalued each year in order to determine the payout amount. Additional contributions can be made to the trust in later years, if desired.

The CRUT may be drafted to pay out less than the established percentage, if the income earned during the year is less than the required payout percentage. This shortage can be made up for in later years when the trust earns more than the required payout percentage.

ERTA: The initials ERTA stand for Economic Recovery Tax Act which was enacted in 1981 and created the unlimited marital tax deduction (which means no estate taxes are paid on the transfer of assets from one spouse to another) and the $10 thousand per year gift tax exemption. In later years the estate tax exemption on transfers of assets from one generation to another was raised from $225 thousand to $600 thousand.

Estate Tax: When property or assets are transferred from one generation to another at death, a tax is imposed on the value of the property and must be paid by those who inherit the estate. This tax is also sometimes referred to as an inheritance tax or death tax.

Executor: The person or institution designated in a will to administer the affairs and finances contained within it.

Family or Credit Shelter Trust: To avoid wasting one spouse's Unified Estate and Gift Tax Credit upon his or her death, it is recommended that the $600 thousand tax exempt amount which each spouse is entitled to, not be transferred to the estate of the remaining spouse. If that $600 thousand comes into the estate of the surviving spouse, his or her heirs will only receive one $600 thousand credit. This can be avoided by using a Family or Credit Shelter Trust. By doing so, when the first spouse dies, his or her $600 thousand credit is placed in a trust which is separate from the surviving spouse's estate. The surviving spouse retains access to virtually all assets and income held within the trust but whatever portion remains upon his or her death passes to the trust's beneficiaries estate tax free.

Generation Skipping Transfer Tax Exemption: The generation skipping transfer tax (GST) is imposed at a flat 55% rate on transfers that skip a generation. Those transfers include "direct skips", where a grandparent transfers property to a grandchild, as well as "taxable terminations" and "taxable distributions", where the child holds an interest in the property before it passes to the grandchild. Even though the GST is computed at a 55% rate, each Grantor has a $1 million exemption for transfers that would otherwise trigger the GST, whether the transfers occur during the Grantor's lifetime or at death. In addition, each Grantor has a $10 thousand annual GST exclusion for each transferee. The two exemptions, in combination, allow a Grantor to make significant property transfers to grandchildren, particularly when those transfers are made with life insurance.

Generation Skipping Trust: Also known as a Dynasty Trust, a generation skipping trust is a legal entity which may be set up outside the estate of the Grantor. Unlike other Trusts which are dissolved upon the death of the Grantor, a generation skipping Trust remains intact throughout multiple generations. The principal amounts held within the Trust remain within it to be passed on from generation to generation yet the assigned Trustees in each generation may distribute the income generated by the Trust's assets to that generation's beneficiaries. Generation skipping trusts may possibly remain in effect for over 100 years.

Gift Tax: When property is transferred from one party to another during life, the value of the property transferred is assessed and taxed.

Grantor: The legal term for any person who creates or establishes a trust for the purpose of transferring property. In some instances, this person may also be referred to as a Trustor which is a synonymous term.

Grantor Retained Income Trust (GRIT): Traditional GRITs were eliminated by Congress in 1990 and replaced with the "Qualified Personal Residence Trust (QPRT)". This trust serves to allow people to place their home into a trust for a set period in order to pass the asset to their heirs with as little transfer tax as possible. The trust exists for a set period of time during which the Grantors may live in the house rent free. At the end of the period of time, the Grantors may either buy the home back from the trust or allow it to pass to the heirs.

Grantor Retained Annuity/Unitrust Trusts (GRAT/GRUT): Similar to a GRIT, the GRAT/GRUT allows the Grantor to retain an interest in the trust for an established period of time. It is different however in that the Grantor receives a fixed amount or percentage of the trust's assets each year.

Immediate Annuity: A financial vehicle purchased with a single up-front principal payment. The principal which purchases the annuity is not recoverable but this allows the annuity to pay significantly higher rates than other investment vehicles. Rates of return are determined by the actuarial assessment of how long the income will be received and, therefore, immediate annuities pay larger returns the older or more ill a person may be.

Illiquid/Illiquidity: Refers to a financial state in which the primary assets are not immediately available as cash. Real estate holdings, businesses, collectibles, etc., are examples of illiquid financial vehicles.

Internal Rate of Return: Used to compare investments, the internal rate of return refers to the percentage of return calculated over the length of time needed to earn the return. The internal rate of return is largely inconsequential as it applies to life insurance purchased for estate tax planning purposes since the insurance's return is guaranteed and the moment of death is unknowable.

Irrevocable Trust: A legal entity which is created to be separate from the estate of the Grantor who establishes it. Once created, the irrevocable trust cannot be revoked by the Grantor; all property placed within the trust remains outside the Grantor's access. The irrevocable trust is especially useful in estate planning as a repository for life insurance proceeds (often referred to as an Irrevocable Life Insurance Trust) since those proceeds do not enter the Grantor's estate and therefore avoid estate taxation. Virtually any asset can be gifted to the trust.

Joint Tenancy: This is a method whereby title to assets or property are held in common between two people. Upon the death of one of the owners, that person's interest in the property passes to the surviving person without the necessity of probate.

Last-to-Die Insurance Policy: This is a type of insurance policy which pays its death benefit following the death of the second of two named people.

Life-Pay: Refers to an on-going method of payment for insurance premiums whereby the policy cost is financed and paid in annual premiums over a lifetime. Like any financed purchase, the total cost of the life-pay premiums includes an interest payment which makes the ultimate cost of the policy higher than it would be if a single, upfront payment were made.

Liquid/Liquidity: That financial state in which a significant portion of your total holdings are held in cash equivalent vehicles such as CD's, T-bills, Municipal Bonds, etc., which can easily be transferred to cash at pre-determined values.

Living (inter vivos) Trust: A legal entity created to avoid the probate process by assigning the distribution of property to occur at death. A Living Trust can be altered by the Grantor during his or her lifetime and therefore does not exist outside his or her estate. For this reason it is subject to estate taxation and is not effectively utilized as a repository for life insurance proceeds.

Margin: A loan from your stock broker against the stocks or bonds in your portfolio.

Marital Deduction: Any assets or property transferred between spouses are subject to an "Unlimited Marital Deduction" which means there are no transfer, gift or estate taxes levied on the transfer regardless of the amount or value of the transferred property.

Modified Endowment: Life insurance policies issued after June 21, 1988 may be defined as modified endowment contracts (MEC), if the cumulative premiums paid during the first seven years at any time exceed the total of the "net level premiums" for the same period.

Withdrawals from "modified endowment contracts" (including loans) will be taxed as current income until all of the policy earnings have been taxed. There is also a 10% penalty tax if the owner is under age 59 ½, unless payments are due to disability or are annuity type payments.

One-Pay: A means of paying an insurance policy premium in one single payment. This method of payment avoids the interest costs inherent in financed policies paid over time. The one payment cost is determined based on current assumptions and can require additional payments down the road if the assumptions change in such a way that your premium is no longer sufficient.

Probate: The literal definition of probate refers to the process of proving that a will is genuine and legitimate. In actuality, probate has come to refer to the process through which an estate must pass following death. In the probate process, the will is reviewed, the assets of the estate are valued and taxes are assessed.

QTIP Trust: A QTIP Trust acts like a Family or Credit Shelter Trust in that in assures that the $600 thousand Unified Estate and Gift Tax Credit of the first spouse to die is kept separate from the surviving spouse's estate and passes to the heirs intact.

Revocable Trust: Any trust over which the Grantor retains control and the ability to make changes or alterations in the terms of the trust or the property contained within it.

Trust: A legal document which creates an entity separate from that of the Grantor into which ownership of property may be transferred with control of that property assigned to a Trustee.

Trustee: The person or institution that manages property within a trust.

BOCA

BASED ON CURRENT ASSUMPTIONS

All figures are based on current assumptions of mortality and interest; any change could affect the cash value, death benefit or outlay as indicated on the proposal.

BOCT

BASED ON CURRENT TAXES

All figures are based on current income taxes. Any changes in the income tax laws will impact this program, producing a higher or lower after tax yield.

BOLE

BASED ON LIFE EXPECTANCY

All figures are based on current life expectancy. This term denotes a period for which the annuitant will be taxed on the interest alone. After such period the annuitant will be taxed on the entire income.

FAT · POLICY · THIN

THE MOST INSURANCE FOR THE LEAST MONEY

Give the insurance company the least amount of money for the most insurance. Only if you are sophisticated and understand you have left no margin for interest drop. Any rise in interest can make a thin policy fat and a fat policy obese.

All figures are based on current assumptions. Charts are for illustrative purposes only.

©1994 WEALTH CREATION CENTERS℠ - Barry Kaye Associates

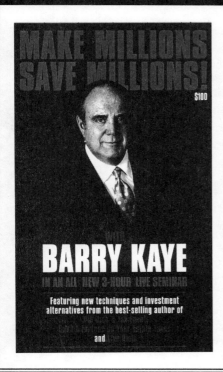